JEREMIAH
and
LAMENTATIONS

J. Vernon McGee

THOMAS NELSON PUBLISHERS

Nashville • Atlanta • London • Vancouver

Published in Nashville, Tennessee, by Thomas Nelson, Inc.

Scripture quotations are from the KING JAMES VERSION of the Bible.

Library of Congress Cataloging-in-Publication Data

McGee, J. Vernon (John Vernon), 1904–1988
   [Thru the Bible with J. Vernon McGee]
   Thru the Bible commentary series / J. Vernon McGee.
     p.   cm.
   Reprint. Originally published: Thru the Bible with J. Vernon McGee. 1975.
   Includes bibliographical references.
   ISBN 0-7852-1025-3 (TR)
   ISBN 0-7852-1085-7 (NRM)
   1. Bible—Commentaries. I. Title.
BS491.2.M37   1991
220.7'7—dc20   90–41340
                                         CIP

Printed in the United States of America

8 9 — 99

CONTENTS

JEREMIAH

LAMENTATIONS

PREFACE

The radio broadcasts of the Thru the Bible Radio five-year program were transcribed, edited, and published first in single-volume paperbacks to accommodate the radio audience.

There has been a minimal amount of further editing for this publication. Therefore, these messages are not the word-for-word recording of the taped messages which went out over the air. The changes were necessary to accommodate a reading audience rather than a listening audience.

These are popular messages, prepared originally for a radio audience. They should not be considered a commentary on the entire Bible in any sense of that term. These messages are devoid of any attempt to present a theological or technical commentary on the Bible. Behind these messages is a great deal of research and study in order to interpret the Bible from a popular rather than from a scholarly (and too-often boring) viewpoint.

We have definitely and deliberately attempted "to put the cookies on the bottom shelf so that the kiddies could get them."

The fact that these messages have been translated into many languages for radio broadcasting and have been received with enthusiasm reveals the need for a simple teaching of the whole Bible for the masses of the world.

I am indebted to many people and to many sources for bringing this volume into existence. I should express my especial thanks to my secretary, Gertrude Cutler, who supervised the editorial work; to Dr. Elliott R. Cole, my associate, who handled all the detailed work with the publishers; and finally, to my wife Ruth for tenaciously encouraging me from the beginning to put my notes and messages into printed form.

Solomon wrote, ". . . of making many books there is no end; and much study is a weariness of the flesh" (Eccl. 12:12). On a sea of books that flood the marketplace, we launch this series of THRU THE BIBLE with the hope that it might draw many to the one Book, *The Bible*.

J. VERNON McGEE

JEREMIAH

The Book of
JEREMIAH

INTRODUCTION

Jeremiah, the prophet of the broken heart, is the writer of this book. It is one of the most remarkable books in the Bible. Every book in the Bible is remarkable, but this book is remarkable in a very unusual way. Most of the prophets hide themselves and maintain a character of anonymity. They do not project themselves on the pages of their prophecy. But Jeremiah is a prophet whose prophecy is largely autobiographical. He gives to us much of his own personal history. Let me run through this list of facts about him so that you will know this man whom we will meet in this book.

1. He was born a priest in Anathoth, just north of Jerusalem (Jer. 1:1).

2. He was chosen to be a prophet before he was born (Jer. 1:5).

3. He was called to the prophetic office while he was very young (Jer. 1:6).

4. He was commissioned of God to be a prophet (Jer. 1:9–10).

5. He began his ministry during the reign of King Josiah and was a mourner at his funeral (2 Chron. 35:25).

6. He was forbidden to marry because of the terrible times in which he lived (Jer. 16:1–4).

7. He never made a convert. He was rejected by his people (Jer. 11:18–21; 12:6; 18:18), hated, beaten, put in stocks (Jer. 20:1–3), imprisoned, and charged with being a traitor (Jer. 37:11–16).

8. His message broke his own heart (Jer. 9:1).

9. He wanted to resign, but God wouldn't let him (Jer. 20:9).

10. He saw the destruction of Jerusalem and the Babylonian captivity. He was permitted to remain in the land by the captain of the Babylonian forces. When the remnant wanted to flee to Egypt, Jeremiah prophesied against it (Jer. 42:15—43:3); he was forced to go with the remnant to Egypt (Jer. 43:6–7); and he died there. Tradition says that he was stoned by the remnant.

Jeremiah was a remarkable man. I call him God's crybaby, but not in a derogatory sense. He was a man in tears most of the time. God chose this man who had a mother's heart, a trembling voice, and tear-filled eyes to deliver a harsh message of judgment. The message that he gave broke his own heart. Jeremiah was a great man of God. Candidly, I don't think that you and I would have chosen this kind of man to give a harsh message. Instead we would have selected some hard-boiled person to give a hard-boiled message, would we not? God didn't choose that kind of man; He chose a man with a tender, compassionate heart.

Lord Macaulay said this concerning Jeremiah: "It is difficult to conceive any situation more painful than that of a great man, condemned to watch the lingering agony of an exhausted country, to tend it during the alternate fits of stupefaction and raving which precede its dissolution, and to see the symptoms of vitality disappear one by one, till nothing is left but coldness, darkness, and corruption" (*Studies in the Prophecy of Jeremiah*, W. G. Moorehead, p. 9). This was the position and the call of Jeremiah. He stood by and saw his people go into captivity.

Dr. Moorehead has given us this very graphic picture of him: "It was Jeremiah's lot to prophesy at a time when all things in Judah were rushing down to the final and mournful catastrophe; when political excitement was at its height; when the worst passions swayed the various parties, and the most fatal counsels prevailed. It was his to stand in the way over which his nation was rushing headlong to destruction; to make an heroic effort to arrest it, and to turn it back; and to fail, and be compelled to step to one side and see his own people, whom he loved with the tenderness of a woman, plunge over the precipice into the wide, weltering ruin" (pages 9, 10).

You and I are living at a time which is probably like the time of

Jeremiah. Ours is a great nation today, and we have accomplished many things. We have gone to the moon, and we have produced atom bombs. Although we are a strong nation, within is the same corruption which will actually carry us down to dismemberment and disaster. It is coming, my friend. Revolution may be just around the corner. I know that what I am saying is not popular today. We don't hear anything like this through the media. Instead, we have panels of experts who discuss how we are going to improve society and how we can work out our problems. Today God is left out of the picture totally—absolutely left out. If the Bible is mentioned, it is mentioned with a curled lip by some unbeliever. The ones who are believers and have a message from God are pushed aside. I *know* that. That is why I say to you that I think we are in very much the same position that Jeremiah was in. For that reason I know this book is going to have a message for us today.

Another author has written, "He was not a man mighty as Elijah, eloquent as Isaiah, or seraphic as Ezekiel, but one who was timid and shrinking, conscious of his helplessness, yearning for a sympathy and love he was never to know—such was the chosen organ through which the Word of the Lord came to that corrupt and degenerate age."

"When Jesus came into the coasts of Caesarea Philippi, he asked his disciples, saying, Whom do men say that I the Son of man am? And they said, Some say that thou art John the Baptist: some, Elias; and others, Jeremias, or one of the prophets" (Matt. 16:13–14). There was a difference of opinion, and none of them seemed to really know who He was. Folk had some good reasons for thinking He was Elijah and also good reasons for thinking He was John the Baptist. Now there were those who thought He was Jeremiah, and they had a very good reason for believing it, because Jeremiah was a man of sorrows and acquainted with grief. The difference between him and the Lord Jesus was that the Lord Jesus was bearing *our* sorrows and *our* grief, while Jeremiah was carrying his *own* burden, and it was breaking his heart. He went to the Lord one time and said, "I can't keep on. This thing is tearing me to pieces. I'm about to have a nervous breakdown. You had better get somebody else." The Lord said, "All right, but I'll just hold your resignation here on My desk because I think you'll be back." Jeremiah did come back, and he said, "The Word of God was like fire in my bones; I had to give it out." He did that even though it broke his heart. God wanted that kind of man, because he was the right kind of man to give a harsh message. God wanted the children of Israel to know that, although He was sending them into captivity and He was judging them, it was breaking *His* heart. As Isaiah says, judgment is God's *strange* work (see Isa. 28:21).

Jeremiah began his ministry about a century after Isaiah. He began his work during the reign of King Josiah, and he continued right on through the Babylonian captivity. He is the one who predicted the seventy years' captivity in Babylon. He also saw beyond the darkness of the captivity to the light. No other prophet spoke so glowingly of the future. We will have occasion to see that as we study his marvelous prophecy.

The message of Jeremiah was the most unwelcome message ever delivered to a people, and it was rejected. He was called a traitor to his country because he said that they were to yield to Babylon. Isaiah, almost a century before him, had said to resist. Why this change? In Jeremiah's day there was only one thing left to do: surrender. In the economy of God, the nation was through. The times of the Gentiles had already begun with Babylon as the head of gold (see Dan. 2).

Characterizing Jeremiah's message is the word *backsliding*, which occurs thirteen times. It is a word that is used only four other times in the Old Testament, once in Proverbs and three times in Hosea—Hosea's message is also that of the backsliding nation.

The name that predominates is *Babylon*, which occurs 164 times in the book, more than in the rest of Scripture combined. Babylon became the enemy.

OUTLINE

I. **Call of Prophet during Reign of Josiah, Chapter 1**

II. **Prophecies to Judah and Jerusalem Prior to Zedekiah's Reign, Chapters 2—20**
   A. Twofold Condemnation of Judah, Chapters 2—3:5
      1. They Rejected Jehovah
      2. They Reared Their Own Gods
   B. Charge of Backsliding during the Reign of Josiah, Chapters 3:6—6
   C. Warning Delivered in Gate of the Lord's House, Chapters 7—10
   D. Israel Disobeyed God's Covenant Made in Wilderness, Chapters 11—12
   E. Parable in Action—the Linen Girdle, Chapter 13
   F. Backsliding Nation Judged by Drought and Famine, Chapters 14—15
   G. Jeremiah Forbidden to Marry, Chapters 16—17:18
   H. Message to King in Gate, Chapters 17:19—27
   I. Sign at Potter's House, Chapters 18—19
   J. Jeremiah's Persecution, Chapter 20

III. **Prophecies during Reign of Zedekiah, Chapters 21—29**
   A. Answer to Zedekiah Regarding Nebuchadnezzar, Chapters 21—22
   B. Bright Light in a Very Dark Day, Chapter 23
   C. Parable of Two Baskets of Figs, Chapter 24
   D. God Spells out Seventy-Year Captivity, Chapter 25
   E. Message in Temple Court during Reign of Jehoiakim, Chapter 26
   F. Parables of Yokes, Chapters 27—28
   G. Message of Hope to First Delegation of Captives, Chapter 29

CHAPTER 1

THEME: Call of prophet during reign of Josiah

It will help our understanding of the prophets to weave them into 1 Samuel through 2 Chronicles, the historical books which cover the same period of time. The prophets prophesied during the time period covered by those historical books—with the exception of Haggai, Zechariah, and Malachi, who prophesied after the Exile (and fit into the time period of the historical Books of Ezra and Nehemiah).

The words of Jeremiah the son of Hilkiah, of the priests that were in Anathoth in the land of Benjamin [Jer. 1:1].

Here is a reference to "Hilkiah" who is the father of Jeremiah. He was the high priest who found the Book of the Law during the time of Josiah. It was the finding of the Law of the Lord as given to Moses that sparked the revival during the reign of Josiah. Revivals are not caused by men; they are caused by the Word of God. Never a man, but the Book. The Word of God is responsible for every revival that has taken place in the church. It is true that God has used men, but it is the Word of God that brings revival. The record of this revival and its effect is found in the historical books in 2 Kings 22 and in 2 Chronicles 34.

"Anathoth" was the hometown of Jeremiah. It is a few miles directly north of Jerusalem.

To whom the word of the Lord came in the days of Josiah the son of Amon king of Judah, in the thirteenth year of his reign [Jer. 1:2].

Josiah was eight years old when he came to the throne, and he reigned for thirty-one years. Jeremiah began his ministry when Josiah was twenty-two years old. Apparently Jeremiah was about twenty years old himself; so both of them were young men and were probably friends. Jeremiah prophesied during eighteen years of Josiah's reign, and he was a mourner at his funeral (see 1 Chron. 35:25).

Josiah had done a very foolish thing—even men of God sometimes do foolish things. He went over to fight against the pharaoh of Egypt at Carchemish although the pharaoh had not come up against Judah at all. For some reason Josiah went out to fight against him in the valley of Esdraelon or Armageddon at Megiddo, and there Josiah was slain. Jeremiah mourned over his death because Josiah had been a good king. The last revival that came to these people came under the reign of Josiah, and it was a great revival. After the death of Josiah, Jeremiah could see that the nation would lapse into a night out of which it would not emerge until after the Babylonian captivity.

It came also in the days of Jehoiakim the son of Josiah king of Judah, unto the end of the eleventh year of Zedekiah the son of Josiah king of Judah, unto the carrying away of Jerusalem captive in the fifth month [Jer. 1:3].

This and the preceding verse give to us the exact time of the ministry of Jeremiah—from the thirteenth year of the reign of Josiah and continuing through the carrying away of Jerusalem into captivity.

We know that when Judah went into captivity, Nebuchadnezzar allowed Jeremiah to stay in the land: "Now Nebuchadnezzar king of Babylon gave charge concerning Jeremiah to Nebuzar-adan the captain of the guard, saying, Take him, and look well to him, and do him no harm; but do unto him even as he shall say unto thee" (Jer. 39:11–12). Of course Jeremiah didn't want to go to Babylon with the others—they had rejected his message and were being led away captives as he had predicted. Since Nebuchadnezzar gave him his choice, he chose to stay in the land with the few who remained. However, those fugitives took off and went down to Egypt, doing it against the advice of Jeremiah and taking him with them. In Egypt Jeremiah continued faithfully giving them God's Word.

Second Chronicles 36 fills in the history which is omitted. Jehoahaz, a son of Josiah, is not mentioned in Jeremiah's record. He reigned for three months—he didn't even get the throne warm before they eliminated him. Then the king of Egypt placed his brother Eliakim on the throne and changed his name to Jehoiakim. He reigned for eleven years. Jeremiah warned him not to rebel against Nebuchadnezzar, king of Babylon. However, Jehoiakim did not listen to the advice from Jeremiah and was taken captive to Babylon. After the removal of Eliakim, the king of Babylon put Jehoiachin on the throne in Jerusalem. He reigned three months and ten days. He is not mentioned here either because he, too, barely got the throne warm and then was eliminated. Nebuchadnezzar took him captive to Babylon. After that it was Zedekiah, the brother of the father of Jehoiachin, who was placed on the throne at Jerusalem. He reigned eleven years. When Zedekiah rebelled, Nebuchadnezzar came and destroyed Jerusalem, slew the sons of Zedekiah, put out Zedekiah's eyes, and took him captive to Babylon.

All of this sounds very brutal, and it was brutal. But we must remember that Nebuchadnezzar had been very patient with the city of Jerusalem. Also the people there refused to listen to God's warning through Jeremiah.

Jeremiah continued his ministry to the remnant that was left at Jerusalem. After they forced him to go to Egypt with them, he still continued his ministry in Egypt until the time of his death. We can say that two things characterized the life of Jeremiah: weeping and loneliness. They are the marks of his ministry.

Then the word of the LORD came unto me, saying [Jer. 1:4].

The "word of the LORD" came to Jeremiah. I can't emphasize that too much. If you are not prepared to go along with that, you might just as well put the book down. It will have no message for you. This is the Word of God. I don't propose to tell you how God got it through to Jeremiah, but He did get it to him, and it is recorded for us as the Word of God.

Before I formed thee in the belly, I knew thee; and before thou camest forth out of the womb I sanctified thee, and I ordained thee a prophet unto the nations [Jer. 1:5].

I am glad that Jeremiah's mother did not practice abortion—he would never have been born. Many people today are asking, "When is a child a child?" May I say to you, a child is a child at the very moment he is conceived. Read Psalm 139. David says, "My substance was not hid from thee, when I was made in secret, and curiously wrought in the lowest parts of the earth" (Ps. 139:15). That is, he was formed in he womb of his mother; and, at that moment, life began. I am told by a gynecologist that there is tremendous development in the fetus at the very beginning. Abortion is murder, unless it is done to save a life That is the way the Word of God looks at it. God said to Jeremiah "Before you were born, I knew you and I called you."

Now why did God say these things to Jeremiah? My friend, God i: going to ask Jeremiah to give a message to the people of Judah that wil be rejected. Jeremiah is going to be imprisoned because of his stanc for God. His message will break his own heart because he loved his people, and he hated to tell them what was going to come to them.

But God wanted a man like this, a tender man, to bring His message. To the court of old Ahab and Jezebel, God had sent a hard-boiled prophet by the name of Elijah. But before the kingdom of Judah goes into captivity, God wants His people to know that He loves them and that He wants to save them and deliver them. For this reason He chose this man Jeremiah.

Therefore God is saying these things to Jeremiah to encourage him. He said, "I want you to know, Jeremiah, that the important thing is that I am the One who has called you, I have ordained you, and I have sanctified you."

Sanctification simply means "to set aside for the use of God." Those old vessels that were used in the tabernacle and temple—old beaten-up pots and pans which were used in God's service—were called *holy* vessels, *sanctified* vessels. When they looked as if they should be traded in for a new set, why were they called holy? Because they were for the use of God. Anything that is set aside for the use of God is sanctified.

God says, "Before you were born, Jeremiah, I set you aside for My use. So don't worry about the effect of your message. You just give the message."

Frankly, God expects the same of me. I feel very comfortable as I prepare these messages. I'm not pulling any punches; I'm giving the Word of God just as it is. That is my responsibility. I say this kindly, I am not responsible to you; I am responsible to God, and I turn my report in to Him. It is just too bad if what I say does not please you. I'm sorry; I wish it did. When I was still in the active pastorate, people would often say, "My, how people love you!" But you know, in every church there was a little group of dissidents—cantankerous trouble-makers who were not always honest. However, if you are giving out the Word of God, you are responsible to God and set aside for that ministry.

God goes on to say, "I ordained thee a prophet unto the nations." This gave authority to Jeremiah. It offered him encouragement that would help him through many a dark day.

Now here is Jeremiah's response:

Then said I, Ah, Lord GOD! behold, I cannot speak: for I am a child [Jer. 1:6].

Jeremiah was probably about twenty years old at the time, but this verse would not lead you to think so. Actually, he was not a child as we think of a child. "Child" here is the same word that is translated "young man" in Zechariah 2:4: "And said unto him, Run, speak to this young man. . . ." Jeremiah was actually a young man. What he is saying in effect is, "I'm a young, inexperienced fellow. I am not capable of doing such a job. I am not prepared for this."

Have you ever noticed that the man whom God uses is the man who doesn't think he can do it? If you think you can do it today, then I say to you that I don't think God can use you.

A young preacher came in to see me who was absolutely green with jealousy of another man in the same town. He said to me, "I'm a better preacher than he is. I'm a better pastor than he is. I'm a better speaker than he is. I want to know *why* God is using that man and He is not using me! My ministry is falling flat." So I told him, "You *think* you can do it. I happen to know the other man, and he really doesn't believe that he can do it. God always uses that kind of a man. God chooses the weak things of this world."

Jeremiah felt inadequate, unfit, unequipped. Listen to God's answer to him:

> **But the Lord said unto me, Say not, I am a child: for thou shalt go to all that I shall send thee, and whatsoever I command thee thou shalt speak [Jer. 1:7].**

"Whatsoever I command thee thou shalt speak." While there are more liberal pulpits in our country, it is the fundamental churches which are really growing in the size of their congregations. It is in the Bible-believing churches where things are really moving today. The problem in the liberal churches is that the man in the pulpit doesn't believe what he is saying. He is giving out *theories* and *ideas*. He holds panel discussions where he tells what *he thinks*. God says, "You give what I command you to give, and give it with that authority." May I say to you, when you are giving out God's Word, it's very comfortable, it's very wonderful. I love Jeremiah, and I would love to have comforted him. He surely has comforted me.

> **Be not afraid of their faces: for I am with thee to deliver thee, saith the Lord [Jer. 1:8].**

"Be not afraid of their faces." One of the comfortable things about my ministry of teaching the Bible on the radio is that my listeners cannot get to me when I say something that displeases them. I heard from a man in Oakland, California, who is now a wonderful Christian. He wrote that he had belonged to a certain cult which believed in certain rituals and gyrations that he had to go through in order to be saved. He would hear our broadcast when he was driving to his work as a contractor. He said, "You made me so mad. You kept telling me I was a sinner. If I could have gotten to you, I would have punched you in the nose." He is a big fellow; so I think he could have done it. That is one reason it is comfortable to be on radio, because when I stay true to the Word of God, I will say things that people don't like to hear. The interesting thing is that this man kept listening morning after morning, and one day he turned to the Lord Jesus and said, "I am a sinner, save me." He accepted Christ as his personal Savior. That is the joy of giving out the Word of God. That is why God says to go ahead and give out His Word with courage and with conviction—it will never return void; it will accomplish God's purpose.

Our pulpits today desperately need men to speak with authority what God has written down in His Word. That is all He asks us to do. It is a simple task in one way, and in another it is a most difficult task.

God says to Jeremiah, "Be not afraid . . . for I am with thee to deliver thee." He is saying, "Look, I am on your side." Martin Luther said, "One with God is a majority." That is always true. As Christians we may feel that we are in the minority, but we really are in the majority.

Then the LORD put forth his hand, and touched my mouth. And the LORD said unto me, Behold, I have put my words in thy mouth [Jer. 1:9].

"I have put my words in thy mouth." This is very important. God has inspired the *words* of Scripture—not just the thoughts and ideas of Scripture. For example, the Devil was not inspired by God to tell a lie, but the record in Scripture that the Devil told a lie is inspired.

This idea is too often misunderstood in our day, which is the reason I cannot commend certain so-called translations of the Bible. They may be good interpretations, but they are very poor translations—because the very words of Scripture are inspired.

Let me illustrate the importance of accurate translation. There was a girl who aspired to be a singer, and the time for her recital had come. After her recital performance she went back to the dressing room where she was met by friends. She eagerly asked, "What did my teacher say?" A very diplomatic friend replied, "He said that you sang *heavenly*." She said, "Did he really say that? Did he say that in so many words?" "Well, that was not exactly the word he used, but that's what he meant," the friend responded. "But I want to know exactly the words he used. Did he say that I sang *heavenly*?" she persisted.

"Well," the friend answered, "he meant that, but what he really said was that it was an *unearthly* noise."

You see it is very important to realize that the words of Scripture are inspired by God. God said to Jeremiah, "I'm going to put *My words* in your mouth."

See, I have this day set thee over the nations and over the kingdoms, to root out, and to pull down, and to destroy, and to throw down, to build, and to plant [Jer. 1:10].

Jeremiah prophesied during the reigns of Josiah, Jehoiakim, Jehoahaz, Jehoiachin, and Zedekiah. All these kings had various bureaus and government projects. They were all going to improve Jerusalem. They were going to deal with the ecology and get rid of the slums. They each had a poverty program. But none of them paid much attention to Jeremiah—they ignored him. Now almost three thousand years have passed by. Could you mention any of those government projects today? Can you tell me anything worthwhile that was done by Zedekiah? Can you mention anything that Jehoiachin or Jehoiakim did? Not a good thing is mentioned. Yet in their day everybody thought they were doing the right thing, the popular thing. Jeremiah was ignored. But whom do we read today? We read Jeremiah.

The Book of Jeremiah is the Word of God, my friend. It has survived and is going to survive through our day. America is a nation that no longer hears God. They don't listen to Him in Washington, D.C. They are not hearing Him in the classrooms of our universities today. And they are not hearing God in the military. The scientists do not listen to Him. But God is speaking and His Word will survive.

God is telling Jeremiah that He is going to put him in charge of giving His Word to the nation of Judah. And poor little Jeremiah wants to retire before he even gets the job!

God now gives Jeremiah two tremendous pictures concerning his call to the prophetic office.

Moreover the word of the LORD came unto me, saying, Jeremiah, what seest thou? And I said, I see a rod of an almond tree [Jer. 1:11].

The almond tree was known as the "waker" or the "watcher." It was actually the first tree to come out of the long night of winter and bloom in the spring. Like the almond tree, Jeremiah was to be an alarm clock—an awaker. He was going to try to wake people up, but they didn't want to be awakened. No one who is asleep likes to be wakened. An alarm clock is one of the most unpopular things in the world. In my college dormitory every alarm clock was battered up; I threw mine against the wall many a morning. Jeremiah is going to be a "waker" to the nation of Judah.

> **Then said the LORD unto me, Thou hast well seen: for I will hasten my word to perform it [Jer. 1:12].**

God said, "That's right. I will give you a word that will wake them up. It will shake them out of sleep."

> **And the word of the LORD came unto me the second time, saying, What seest thou? And I said, I see a seething pot; and the face thereof is toward the north [Jer. 1:13].**

What was the "seething pot"? In Jeremiah's time Egypt and Assyria were no longer a danger to the southern kingdom of Judah, but around the Fertile Crescent in the north was a boiling pot: the rising power of Babylon, which was to eventually destroy Judah. It was to be Jeremiah's job to constantly warn his people what was going to happen to their nation.

> **The the LORD said unto me, Out of the north an evil shall break forth upon all the inhabitants of the land.**
>
> **For, lo, I will call all the families of the kingdoms of the north, saith the LORD; and they shall come, and they shall set every one his throne at the entering of the gates of Jerusalem, and against all the walls thereof round about, and against all the cities of Judah [Jer. 1:14–15].**

A century earlier God had delivered Jerusalem, and now all the false prophets were running around saying that He was going to do it again.

All of God's prophets of the past—Hosea, Joel, Amos, Micah and Nahum, all those who had been contemporaries of Isaiah—had now passed off the scene. I think Zephaniah and Habakkuk were still living. Ezekiel and Obadiah were also contemporary with Jeremiah, but they were not going to prophesy until the captives are actually in Babylon. Daniel, too, will be prophesying later on. But at this time, Jeremiah stands alone, and he is to utter these judgments that are to come upon the nation.

What will be the reaction to his message?—

> **And they shall fight against thee; but they shall not prevail against thee; for I am with thee, saith the LORD, to deliver thee [Jer. 1:19].**

The Lord says, "Go ahead, Jeremiah, they're going to resist you, they won't listen to the message, but you give the message." Jeremiah feels incapable and unworthy of the office of prophet, and he has offered that as an excuse. But God says, "I'm going to put My words in your mouth, and you will be giving My words."

I do not believe that any man ought to stand in the pulpit and give a message until he is sure that he is giving the Word of God. If he has any doubts or if he feels that he should give his own ideas and preach a liberal, social gospel—he ought to stay out of the pulpit. Regardless of how much homiletics, or hermeneutics, or theology, or sophisticated training he has had, unless he is confident that he is giving the Word of God, he ought to stay out of the pulpit. That is very important. Jeremiah could be confident that he was giving out the very words of God.

CHAPTER 2

THEME: Twofold condemnation of Judah

In the first chapter we saw the impressive call and commission of Jeremiah. God called him when he was a young man, probably about twenty years of age. We know also that the king Josiah was twenty-one or twenty-two years old when God called Jeremiah. So here we have two young men in the land of Israel, the young king and the young prophet.

Jeremiah made it very clear that he felt incapable and unworthy of such a calling. He felt that he could not measure up to the office of a prophet, and he offered that as an excuse. God answered him that He would put His words into Jeremiah's mouth. He would be giving God's words, not his own.

Chapters 2 through 6 were given during the first five years of Jeremiah's ministry. And since he began to prophesy in the thirteenth year of the reign of Josiah, these messages were given in those five years before the finding of the Book of the Law in the temple. The messages in chapters 7 through 9 have to do with the cleansing of the temple and the discovery of the Book of the Law, which took place in the eighteenth years of the reign of Josiah. Then in chapters 10 through 12 are the messages which came in the period of reform and revival *after* the finding of the Book of the Law. We will discover that the revival was a surface sort of thing because there was not proper emphasis placed upon the Word of God.

Friend, we need to remember that there will never be a real revival until there is a real emphasis placed upon the Word of God.

In order to orient ourselves for this period of history, we need to study the historical books along with the prophetic books. Therefore we will turn back to the thirty-fourth chapter of 2 Chronicles to fit the messages of Jeremiah into this particular place in history: "Josiah was eight years old when he began to reign, and he reigned in Jerusalem one and thirty years. And he did that which was right in the sight of the LORD, and walked in the ways of David his father, and declined neither to the right hand, nor to the left" (2 Chron. 34:1–2). Here is an outstanding king who reigned during the twilight of the kingdom of Judah.

"For in the eighth year of his reign, while he was yet young, he began to seek after the God of David his father: and in the twelfth year he began to purge Judah and Jerusalem from the high places, and the groves, and the carved images, and the molten images (2 Chron. 34:3). Jeremiah's first five years of prophesying were during this period.

"And they brake down the altars of Baalim in his presence; and the images, that were on high above them, he cut down; and the groves, and the carved images, and the molten images, he brake in pieces, and made dust of them, and strowed it upon the graves of them that had sacrificed unto them. And he burnt the bones of the priests upon their altars, and cleansed Judah and Jerusalem. And so did he in the cities of Manasseh, and Ephraim, and Simeon, even unto Naphtali, with their mattocks round about. And when he had broken down the altars and the groves, and had beaten the graven images into powder, and cut down all the idols throughout all the land of Israel, he returned to Jerusalem. Now in the eighteenth year of his reign, when he had purged the land, and the house, he sent Shaphan the son of Azaliah, and Maaseiah the governor of the city, and Joah the son of Joahaz the recorder, to repair the house of the LORD his God" (2 Chron. 34:4–8). It was during this time of cleaning out and repairing the house of the Lord that Hilkiah the priest found a Book of the Law as it had been given to Moses. In those days probably there were only two copies—one was for the king and one was for the high priest. You see, before Josiah had come to the throne, Judah had sunk to a new low under the wicked and godless reins of his grandfather, Manasseh, and his father, Amon. They had no regard for God or His Word, and the one or two copies in existence were finally lost in the rubbish which collected in the neglected temple.

Jeremiah's first message (2:1—3:5) is to this people who had forsaken the living God. It would be difficult to find any portion of Scripture that would surpass it in genuine pathos and tenderness. It is the eloquent and earnest pleading of a God who has been forgotten and insulted. His grace and compassion toward the guilty nation are blended with solemn warnings of dreadful days to come if hearts are not turned back to Him. This is one of the great discourses in the Word of God. The young king Josiah was truly seeking the Lord, but he didn't have the Word of God! He did know, however, that idolatry must be put down. Now he has a young man, a young prophet, who will encourage him in his resolve.

THEY REJECTED JEHOVAH

Moreover the word of the LORD came to me, saying,

Go and cry in the ears of Jerusalem, saying, Thus saith the LORD; I remember thee, the kindness of thy youth, the love of thine espousals, when thou wentest after me in the wilderness, in a land that was not sown.

Israel was holiness unto the LORD, and the firstfruits of his increase: all that devour him shall offend; evil shall come upon them, saith the LORD [Jer. 2:1–3].

God is doing something quite wonderful. He is asking Israel to remember the springtime of their relationship to Him when He called them out of the land of Egypt—how they followed the pillar of fire at night and the pillar of cloud by day. Out in that frightful and terrible wilderness they sought the Lord. God now reminds them of that. After God had blessed them and given them a good land, they turned from Him. As Hosea had said of the northern kingdom, "Ephraim waxed fat and wicked." In their comfortable and sophisticated society, they turned away from the living God to serve idols.

One cannot help but note that there is an analogy between Judah and our own nation. God is left out today. Our nation was founded by men and women who believed that the Book was the Word of God, and everything they did was based on that Book. As one of our outstanding historians has observed, our nation is controlled by men who do not know its spiritual heritage. We have turned away from God. We are going after the idol of the almighty dollar. The best news out of New York is a vigorous stock market. The best news out of Washington is that which will put more money in our pockets. Money is the god of the present hour. The Ephesians chanted, ". . . Great is Diana of the Ephesians" (Acts 19:28). The cry of America is, "Great is the almighty American dollar," and God is left out.

"I remember thee." God says, "I remember you." They had forgotten Him, but God had not forgotten them. Oh, how gracious God is!

Listen to His longing: "Israel was holiness unto the LORD. Don't you remember back there how you were? You belonged to Me. You followed Me and you were led by Me."

> **Here ye the word of the LORD, O house of Jacob, and all the families of the house of Israel [Jer. 2:4].**

Although the ten tribes had been conquered by the Assyrians, they were still around. They hadn't wandered over to Great Britain or America. He addresses the house of Jacob and *all* the families of Israel. (And they are the same people today, by the way.) God's message was to them in that day although they were in the Assyrian captivity.

> **Thus saith the LORD, What iniquity have your fathers found in me, that they are gone far from me, and have walked after vanity, and are become vain? [Jer. 2:5].**

Without doubt this is one of the great passages of Scripture. Notice the wonderful way in which God approaches them: "What did I do wrong that you have turned from Me?"

In our day, my friend, what is wrong with God that we are not more interested in Him? Why are we not serving Him? Is there unrighteousness with God? Is God doing something wrong today? He asks, "What iniquity have your fathers found in me?"

> **Neither said they, Where is the LORD that brought us up out of the land of Egypt, that led us through the wilderness, through a land of deserts and of pits, through a**

land of drought, and of the shadow of death, through a land that no man passed through, and where no man dwelt? [Jer. 2:6].

People just didn't go through that country, and there are not many who go through that country today. I have been at the edge of it, and that is as far as I have wanted to go. Yet God kept His people in that frightful wilderness for forty years, and He took care of them.

And I brought you into a plentiful country, to eat the fruit thereof and the goodness thereof; but when ye entered, ye defiled my land, and made mine heritage an abomination [Jer. 2:7].

Today we hear a great deal about ecology and the fact that we need to clean up the land. That is good—it needs cleaning up. But let's recognize that there is a lot of moral filth around and a lot of degradation and deterioration in character. This is the thing that the Lord God is talking about here. They had polluted God's land. God intended that they be a witness to Him; instead, they are as bad as the people before them.

The priests said not, Where is the LORD? and they that handle the law knew me not: the pastors also transgressed against me, and the prophets prophesied by Baal, and walked after things that do not profit [Jer. 2:8].

God puts the responsibility on the spiritual leaders. And I believe that the problems in my country began in the church. No nation falls until it falls first spiritually. There is first of all a spiritual apostasy, then a moral awfulness, and finally a political anarchy. That is the way every nation makes its exit as a great nation.

"The priests said not, Where is the LORD?" There are too many folk today who are supposed to be Bible teachers and preachers and witnesses for Him, even among the laymen, who do not know the Word of

God. I am sorry to say that, but it happens to be true. As a result of not knowing the Word of God, they don't really know God. It is necessary to know the Word of God in order to know Him.

> **Wherefore I will yet plead with you, saith the LORD, and with your children's children will I plead [Jer. 2:9].**

God says, "I have not given you up. I am still going to plead with you." How wonderful that is.

> **For my people have committed two evils; they have forsaken me the fountain of living waters, and hewed them out cisterns, broken cisterns, that can hold no water [Jer. 2:13].**

Israel had committed two evils. First of all, they rejected Jehovah, the fountain of living waters. Second, they hewed out cisterns for themselves, broken cisterns that couldn't hold water.

Oh, how many people today have hewn out a little cistern for themselves, and they drink from their own cistern! Of course they are not finding satisfaction. For example, every man who has made a million dollars thirsts for more—he wants to make the second million. The same is true of fame. There is never enough to satisfy.

God goes on to deal with these people, mentioning their backsliding for the first time.

> **Thine own wickedness shall correct thee, and thy backslidings shall reprove thee: know therefore and see that it is an evil thing and bitter, that thou hast forsaken the LORD thy God, and that my fear is not in thee, saith the Lord GOD of hosts [Jer. 2:19].**

In chapter 3 we will find that backsliding is mentioned in one chapter as many times as it is mentioned in the rest of the Bible; so it must be rather important to God.

THEY REARED THEIR OWN GODS

The remainder of chapter 2 is a polemic against idolatry, which continues in chapter 3. Rather than quote this section, I want to recommend that you read it in your Bible, read it all the way through. As you become familiar with the prophecy of Jeremiah, you will be surprised how wonderful it will become to you.

It is interesting to see that when man rejects God, he always will make an idol. When people make their own god, they make it as they want it. They make a god whose demands they can meet. In other words, it is actually a projection of the old nature of man.

CHAPTER 3

THEME: Josiah begins reforms in the nation

In Jeremiah's first message, begun in chapter 2, God has condemned Judah on two scores: they have rejected Jehovah, and they have reared their own gods. The first five verses of chapter 3 will continue on this theme. The messages found in chapters 2 through 6 were given during the first five years of Jeremiah's ministry before the Book of the Law was found. During this time, however, Josiah, a young man like Jeremiah, was seeking the Lord and instituting certain reforms in the nation. Primarily, he was trying to clean up the idolatry in Judah. The nation had forsaken the living God and had gone over into idolatry. You can see that the combined efforts of this young king and the young prophet Jeremiah had a tremendous effect upon the nation.

Judah had gone over to idolatry because it was the easy way and the popular way, but it was a pathway that led to the lowering of their standards and brought them down to a low moral level.

> **They say, If a man put away his wife, and she go from him, and become another man's, shall he return unto her again? shall not that land be greatly polluted? but thou hast played the harlot with many lovers; yet return again to me, saith the LORD [Jer. 3:1].**

Judah had sunk to a very low level—there was gross immorality in the land. She had played the harlot; yet God asks her to return to Him.

> **Lift up thine eyes unto the high places, and see where thou hast not been lien with. In the ways hast thou sat for them, as the Arabian in the wilderness; and thou hast polluted the land with thy whoredoms and with thy wickedness [Jer. 3:2].**

Idolatry is not simply making a little idol to worship. Anything that a man gives himself to wholeheartedly is idolatry. The Bible teaches that covetousness is idolatry, because when a man covets something, he gives his time, his energy to that—he is dedicated to it. Especially in these last days we see a great many people who are dedicated to sin, and the energy they put into sin is tremendous. But, you see, the minute a man turns away from the living God, he will turn to something else. It will be something he has made, and it becomes his god, his idol.

Dr. G. Campbell Morgan has made this very fine statement about the nature of idolatry and the worship of the true God:

> . . . When a man makes a god according to the pattern of his own being, he makes a god like himself, an enlargement of his own imperfection. Moreover, the god which a man makes for himself will demand from him that which is according to his own nature. It is clearly evident in Mohammedanism. Great and wonderful and outstanding in his personality as Mohammed was, yet the blighting sensuality of the man curses the whole of Islam today. Men will be faithful to those gods who make no demands upon them which are out of harmony with the desires of their own hearts.
>
> When God calls men, it is the call of the God of holiness, the God of purity, the God of love; and He demands that they rise to His height. He cannot accommodate Himself to the depravity of their nature. He will not consent to the things of desire within them that are of impurity and evil. He calls men up, and even higher, until they reach the height of perfect conformity to His holiness. God's call to humanity is always first pure, and then peaceable; first holy, and then happy; first righteous, and then rejoicing (*Studies in the Prophecy of Jeremiah,* p. 36).

God said that Jeremiah's generation in Judah had gone wholeheartedly into idolatry, and as a result there was gross immorality in the land. When He says, "Lift up thine eyes unto the high places," you must understand how grossly immoral those high places were. A high place was a grove of trees where an idolatrous altar had been built. All kinds of sex orgies and drunken revelries were carried on there. Judah had sunk to a very low level.

The comparison to our own nation today is obvious, is it not? America has forsaken the living and true God, which is evident in the moral condition of this country. What lawlessness, dishonesty, and corrupt speech we find everywhere! We have even taught our children the use of very foul language.

> **Therefore the showers have been withholden, and there hath been no latter rain; and thou hadst a whore's forehead, thou refusedst to be ashamed [Jer. 3:3].**

God tells them that He has already begun to judge them by withholding rain. Even today that land is dry. Their greatest need is water—even more than oil. They didn't find oil in the Negeb, but they found water, and that is much more precious to them. I believe that when the Jews return to Israel under the blessing of God, they are going to have all the water they need. God has said that He will supply it.

I think that we can see God's judgment upon our own nation in the many national calamities which we have suffered over the past several years. Unfortunately, it doesn't seem to wake us up and bring us back to Him.

CHARGE OF BACKSLIDING DURING THE REIGN OF JOSIAH

We come now to the second message of Jeremiah. It begins in verse 6 of chapter 3 and extends all the way through chapter 6. In this message God charges the people with backsliding. The word *backsliding* is used seven times in this chapter, and that is more than half the number of times in the entire book. In Jeremiah we find this word more often than in the rest of the Bible put together. He and Hosea are the ones who use it.

Backsliding does not simply mean "to slide backwards" as we usually think of it. God gives us a vivid picture of what He means by backsliding when He tells us, "For Israel slideth back as a backsliding heifer . . ." (Hos. 4:16). Do you have any idea what it is like to try to load calves into a truck or wagon? When I was a boy, we lived next door to a southern Oklahoma rancher. He had two sons who were my friends. (They were mean boys, and I ran with them—but, of course, I was a good boy!) Sometimes we would go out to the ranch and help load the heifers. Do you know what they do when you try to get them up the ramp? They set their front feet and make themselves as stiff as they can. They brace themselves so that you cannot move them at all. When we would try to move them, they would start slipping backwards. That is God's picture of what it means to backslide.

Backsliding is a refusal to go God's way, a refusal to listen to Him. And when we do as the heifers do, when we set our wills against God's will, we wind up going backwards every time. If we rebel against the Lord and His will, we only get farther and farther away from Him.

> **The LORD said also unto me in the days of Josiah the king, Hast thou seen that which backsliding Israel hath done? she is gone up upon every high mountain and under every green tree, and there hath played the harlot [Jer. 3:6].**

God tells Judah to take a lesson from Israel which had already gone into captivity. He tells them to take notice of the fact that Israel had done exactly what they are doing. "Israel slideth back as a backsliding heifer." But God had tried to get Israel to return to Him, and they would not return. As a result they were taken off into captivity. What happened to Israel should serve as a lesson and should be a warning to Judah.

In verse 1 of this chapter God said, "Yet return again to me, saith the LORD." He says, "Though you have played the harlot, you belong to Me. If you come back to Me, I'll receive you." That is the reason any prodigal son or any prodigal daughter or any prodigal family or any prodigal church or any prodigal nation can always come back to God.

God will receive you. The prodigal son didn't get any kicks when he came home. He had gotten those in the far country! He received kisses instead. He had nearly starved in the far country, but his father prepared a banquet for him when he came home.

But Israel had not returned to God. They went into idolatry, and God sent them into captivity. Now He says to Judah, "Let this be a lesson to you."

> **And I said after she had done all these things, Turn thou unto me. But she returned not. And her treacherous sister Judah saw it [Jer. 3:7].**

God says, "I gave Israel an opportunity to turn to me. I would have taken her back, but she wouldn't come. And her treacherous sister Judah saw it." The sin of Judah is compounded. I think her captivity was much worse than that of the ten northern tribes, and the reason is self-evident: Judah had Israel's captivity as an example and refused to profit by it.

The tragedy in this country is that we have a Bible, but very few are reading it. I get a little weary of hearing people say, "We live in a land where we have an open Bible, and we can read the Bible." Well, thank God for that, but who is *reading* it? How many people are really reading it? Judah did not turn to God even though they had an example. You and I have the Word of God today, and therefore I believe God will judge this country more harshly than He will judge nations such as the Soviet Union. They don't have Bibles over there, but you and I do. I believe God will judge us according to the opportunities He gives us.

> **And it came to pass through the lightness of her whoredom, that she defiled the land, and committed adultery with stones and with stocks [Jer. 3:9].**

They made idols of sticks and stones.

> **And yet for all this her treacherous sister Judah hath not turned unto me with her whole heart, but feignedly, saith the LORD [Jer. 3:10].**

The revival under King Josiah was a revival—there is no question about it. Many people turned to God. But it was so popular that for many it was nothing but a surface return to God. By and large, as far as the nation is concerned, it was a superficial experience with God.

I believe that there is a renewed interest in the Word of God today, and I think more people are being saved than at any time during the years of my ministry. But let's be very careful—it is not a revival. A great deal of it is quite surface. Don't be deceived by the large crowds in places or by the number who are reported to have accepted Christ. Just divide that number by two, and you'll probably get the number of those who have been *genuinely* converted. We see a great surface movement as well as that which is genuine.

And the Lord said unto me, The backsliding Israel hath justified herself more than treacherous Judah [Jer. 3:11].

God is making it clear that the sin of Judah is worse than the sin of Israel. The northern tribes didn't have the same opportunity as the southern tribes. They did not have the temple nor did they have a copy of the Word of God. Therefore the judgment on Judah was greater. I believe the judgment on us will be greater also.

Go and proclaim these words toward the north, and say, Return, thou backsliding Israel, saith the Lord; and I will not cause mine anger to fall upon you: for I am merciful, saith the Lord, and I will not keep anger for ever [Jer. 3:12].

God tells Israel that He will bring them back into the land if they will turn to Him. How gracious God is! How wonderful He is!

Only acknowledge thine iniquity, that thou hast transgressed against the Lord thy God, and hast scattered thy ways to the strangers under every green tree, and ye have not obeyed my voice, saith the Lord [Jer. 3:13].

Today the big problem is a lack of confession of sin. I find that repentance is lacking in much of the so-called spiritual movement of today. An example is a book I read recently which disturbed me. The author constantly used the first person pronoun, and the Lord received none of the glory. He told what God had done for him, how He had made him a millionaire, a big success. But I didn't find anywhere a statement that God had saved him from sin. We need to confess our iniquity.

My friend, do you say that you are a Christian? What do you mean by that? Perhaps you say that you have trusted Christ. Trusted Him for *what*? You may say that you trust Him as your Savior. Fine! I'm glad to hear that. Did He save you from *sin*? Remember that He died on the Cross to save you from *sin*, not to give you a new personality or to make you a millionaire. He died to save us all from our sins. He was delivered for our offenses—we were all very offensive to God. The word of God through Jeremiah is "acknowledge thine iniquity," and it is directed to us as well as to Judah.

> **Turn, O backsliding children, saith the Lord; for I am married unto you: and I will take you one of a city, and two of a family, and I will bring you to Zion [Jer. 3:14].**

Oh how gracious God was!

> **And I will give you pastors according to mine heart, which shall feed you with knowledge and understanding [Jer. 3:15].**

My friend, if you have a Bible-teaching pastor, you ought to run over and put your arm around him. You ought to protect him, because he is valuable. Such men are few and far between.

> **And it shall come to pass, when ye be multiplied and increased in the land, in those days, saith the Lord, they shall say no more, The ark of the covenant of the Lord: neither shall it come to mind: neither shall they remem-**

ber it; neither shall they visit it; neither shall that be done any more [Jer. 3:16].

"In those days" is a reference to the millennial Kingdom. All the way through the Book of Jeremiah we will find these rays of light. Have you ever been out on a cloudy day when all of a sudden the sun breaks through and you see a rainbow? This is how it will be throughout Jeremiah—we will have these glorious prophecies of the future.

At that time they shall call Jerusalem the throne of the LORD; and all the nations shall be gathered unto it, to the name of the LORD, to Jerusalem: neither shall they walk any more after the imagination of their evil heart.

In those days the house of Judah shall walk with the house of Israel, and they shall come together out of the land of the north to the land that I have given for an inheritance unto your fathers [Jer. 3:17–18].

This is a glorious prophecy. It is like a little gem.

But I said, How shall I put thee among the children, and give thee a pleasant land, a goodly heritage of the hosts of nations? and I said, Thou shalt call me, My father; and shalt not turn away from me [Jer. 3:19].

"Thou shalt call me, My father." No individual Israelite ever called God his Father. He was a Father to the *nation* of Israel, and He said ". . . Israel is my son . . ." (Exod. 4:22). But he never called David His son; He said, ". . . David my servant" (Ps. 89:3). He never called Moses His son; He called him, "Moses my servant . . ." (Josh. 1:2). It is only in this day of grace that we are called the sons of God. How privileged we are today! "But as many as received him, to them gave he power [the right] to become *the sons of God,* even to them that believe on his name" (John 1:12). Those who do no more and no less than simply trust in His name become the sons of God. Is He your Savior from sin?

If He is, you are not only a saved sinner, you are a son of God. How wonderful that is!

> **Return, ye backsliding children, and I will heal your backslidings. Behold, we come unto thee; for thou art the LORD our God [Jer. 3:22].**

The Lord says that He will heal. I can tell you that you have a little sore in a very prominent place if you do a lot of backsliding my friend. God says, "I will heal you if you will come to Me."

> **Truly in vain is salvation hoped for from the hills, and from the multitude of mountains: truly in the LORD our God is the salvation of Israel [Jer. 3:23].**

In Psalm 121 David says, "I will lift up mine eyes unto the hills, from whence cometh my help. My help cometh from the LORD, which made heaven and earth" (Ps. 121:1–2). Help does not come from those high places on the hills. Salvation comes from the Lord.

> **We lie down in our shame, and our confusion covereth us: for we have sinned against the LORD our God, we and our fathers, from our youth even unto this day, and have not obeyed the voice of the LORD our God [Jer. 3:25].**

Judah did not confess their sins. Jeremiah confessed their sins for them and for himself, also.

You know, it wouldn't hurt for us to have a little confession of sin today. We hear so much about special gifts and about God's blessing in special ways. That is wonderful. We should thank God because He has blessed us. But have you ever heard a confession that we come short of the glory of God? Have you gone to Him yourself and told Him how far you fall short of His glory? We need to be humble before Him.

Judah was not humble before God, and God had to send them into captivity. I often wonder whether the Lord is getting ready to chastise us. We need to be humble before Him.

CHAPTERS 4—6

THEME: *Jeremiah deals with backsliding of the people*

We are in that period of time when Josiah the king was carrying on a reformation, but it was before the Word of God had been found in the temple. Therefore it was reformation and not revival. That which was taking place was very shallow. Josiah was sincere, and he was certainly moved toward God. He listened to Jeremiah. But the people were not turning back to God in any genuine sort of way, even though Jeremiah had struck home in some of the prophecies he had given.

We are in the second message which Jeremiah gave (it began in ch. 3 and continues through ch. 6). He deals with the backsliding of the people. "And yet for all this her treacherous sister Judah hath not turned unto me with her whole heart, but feignedly, saith the LORD" (Jer. 3:10). They were turning to God in a merely outward manner. They were going to the temple and were going through the rituals, but their heart was not in it at all. It was something Josiah was trying to produce. This reveals that there can be reformation without revival. Reformation without revival is never a genuine change.

I am not quite sure that what we are seeing around us as I write this book is true revival. This renewed interest in the Word of God could become revival, but it may be merely an experience jag that a great many people are on at the present. It remains to be seen whether they are genuinely converted or not.

Although in Jeremiah's time there was reformation rather than a real turning to God, it was enough to prompt Jeremiah to give a tremendous prophecy in Jeremiah 3:16–18. He says that "in those days" all the nations will gather to the house of God in Jerusalem. Even that fact should have alerted Judah not to make their temple worship ritualistic, but they did not respond. Yet the Lord continues to plead with them. "Return, ye backsliding children, and I will heal your backslidings" (Jer. 3:22).

At the beginning of chapter 4 we find an expression of the Lord's response to any movement on the part of the people toward Him.

> **If thou wilt return, O Israel, saith the LORD, return unto me: and if thou wilt put away thine abominations out of my sight, then shalt thou not remove [Jer. 4:1].**

He is vitally interested in them, and He wants to bring them back into a right relationship to Himself. He tells them that He will not remove them from the land if they will but turn to Him.

> **And thou shalt swear, The LORD liveth, in truth, in judgment, and in righteousness; and the nations shall bless themselves in him, and in him shall they glory.**
>
> **For thus saith the LORD to the men of Judah and Jerusalem, Break up your fallow ground, and sow not among thorns [Jer. 4:2–3].**

In other words, reformation is no good. You can sow the seed on the ground, but the ground must first be prepared for it. There is no use sowing seed on thorny ground. Our Lord expressed it another way, ". . . neither cast ye your pearls before swine . . ." (Matt. 7:6). I believe there are certain times and certain places where there is no point in giving out the Word of God. There are times when men attempt evangelism because it is spectacular and sensational. God says, "Break up your fallow ground." As Dr. H. A. Ironside has put it, "The plowshare of conviction must overturn the hardened soil of the heart."

In the remainder of this section, there will first be an impeachment of the people. God will pronounce a judgment upon them and will call to them to return to Jehovah. Finally, there will be a clear foretelling of judgment. Believe me, Jeremiah will not mince words about that.

My feeling is that there ought to be more of the message of the prophets rather than the message of comfort in our own day. The fallow ground needs to be broken up. We are a nation in danger. We say we are one of the greatest nations in the world, but we could fall overnight. Babylon the great fell in one night; Alexander the Great died in a night, and his entire empire crumbled; the Roman Empire fell from within, and we can go down just like that. Our greatness does not depend upon our atom bombs or the almighty dollar. We are decaying from within. There is deterioration, moral deterioration. Somebody needs to be saying something about it, but very little is being said. It seems to me that we are sowing seed on ground that is thorny. The Lord warns us against doing that.

God continues to offer to Judah an opportunity to come back to Him.

> **Circumcise yourselves to the LORD, and take away the foreskins of your heart, ye men of Judah and inhabitants of Jerusalem: lest my fury come forth like fire, and burn that none can quench it, because of the evil of your doings [Jer. 4:4].**

They were going through the outward form of circumcision. Circumcision was a badge that showed they belonged to the nation Israel, but God hadn't given it just as a form or a ceremony. Circumcision has been shown to have a very definite therapeutic value, but the important thing was its spiritual value. Their *hearts* needed to be turned to God.

Now Jeremiah lets them know that there will come a power out of the north—that will be Babylon—which will eventually destroy them.

> **Set up the standard toward Zion: retire, stay not: for I will bring evil from the north, and a great destruction.**

> **The lion is come up from his thicket, and the destroyer of the Gentiles is on his way; he is gone forth from his place to make thy land desolate; and thy cities shall be laid waste, without an inhabitant.**

> **For this gird you with sackcloth, lament and howl: for the fierce anger of the LORD is not turned back from us [Jer. 4:6–8].**

Judah had seen the ten tribes of the north go into captivity. Now Jeremiah is asking them to take warning from that. God is raising up a power, a new power in the north, and that power will come down and will finally destroy them.

The natural man cannot produce any righteousness at all. That is why Jeremiah calls the people to a circumcision of their hearts. But we see here that the people refused to turn to God; and, when a nation or a church or an individual rejects God, God rejects them. Remember that the Lord Jesus came and offered Himself as the King to Israel. When they rejected Him, He in turn rejected them. He said to them, "Behold, your house is left unto you desolate" (Matt. 23:38). Read that whole chapter of Matthew 23—if that doesn't make you blanch with fear, nothing will. Don't talk about the gentle Jesus! They rejected Him as their King, and then He rejected them.

Friend, you are free to reject God—that is your free will. But remember, if you reject God, God will reject you. He is gracious; He is good; He is patient and longsuffering; He gives you ample opportunity to turn to Him. But it is sobering to see what happens to any privileged people who refuse God, be it Israel or be it the church. God finally refuses them, and then all other men count them as reprobate, refuse, and worthless.

We have too many people today who give a pretense of being followers of the living and true God. Many of them are members in the churches today. We often hear the expression that we are a Christian nation in America. I say we are not a Christian nation. There is no emphasis on the Word of God, and we are not following the living and true God.

The *Reader's Digest* published an article quite some time ago entitled, "The Book Almost Nobody Reads." Of course, they were referring to the Bible. I agree with that title. But notice what was said: "In short, one way to describe the Bible, written by many different hands over a period of 3,000 years and more, would be to say it is a disorderly collection of 60-odd books which are often tedious, barbaric, obscure and teeming with contradictions and inconsistencies. It is a swarming compost of a book, an Irish stew of poetry and propaganda, law and legalism, myth and murk, history and hysteria." Now that is a *lie*, my friend! The man who wrote the article knows nothing about the content of the Word of God.

I say to you that we are in the same kind of position today as were those people in the days of Jeremiah. The nation at that time had rejected God, but the people were still making a pretense of following Him. Such a people will find themselves rejected by God and by the world. America is following that same path. We are not loved by the world today. After World War II we were the pious people who were going to bring democracy to the world. What have we done? We have brought lawlessness into our own land. Do you think we should bring lawlessness into the trails of the jungle as we have into the streets of our cities? Is that the kind of civilization we are going to bring to people?

We find ourselves despised by other nations. God said it would be that way. No people can pretend to be God-fearing, be hypocritical about it, and still expect the world to look up to them. God has ordered it that way. I know it is not popular to say this—Jeremiah wasn't very popular in his day, either. I am not expecting to win any popularity contest. The chamber of commerce will never elect me to be the man of the year. They would rather give me the boot, I am sure. But I must tell you honestly the message of this Book: A people who turn away from God will find that God turns away from them.

Now let me lift out some high points as we go through this message.

For my people is foolish, they have not known me; they are sottish children, and they have none understanding: they are wise to do evil, but to do good they have no knowledge [Jer. 4:22].

It is interesting to note that our government uses the help of those they call the intellectuals. Perhaps it was Franklin Roosevelt who started this with his "brain trust"—this idea of going to Harvard or some other prestigious university and getting the advice of some of the boys with high IQs. Oh, we are wise in doing evil! We think we have been real clever cookies in our dealings around the world. We think we are big business. We are big in everything but righteousness, my friend. We are not very big on knowing God. God says that those who pretend to know Him and don't really know Him are foolish.

The man who wrote the article that I just quoted was no more competent to write about the Word of God than I am to write about the *Congressional Record* or the Smithsonian Institution! I know nothing about those things. These famous intellectuals who are not real believers are not capable of writing about the Word of God. They do not know God, and you must know *Him* in order to know His Book. It is interesting that you can read a human book and understand it without knowing the author of the book. A human book by a human author can be understood by another human being. But if you want to know the Bible, you need to know the Author and have Him as your Teacher. Only the spirit of God can make the Word of God real to you.

JEREMIAH SPELLS OUT SPECIFIC SINS

Run ye to and fro through the streets of Jerusalem, and see now, and know, and seek in the broad places thereof, if ye can find a man, if there be any that executeth judgment, that seeketh the truth; and I will pardon it [Jer. 5:1].

You remember the story of old Diogenes, the Greek philosopher, who went through the streets of Athens with a lantern. They asked him what he was looking for, and his answer was, "I am looking for an honest man." He never did find one. I think you would have the same trouble in Los Angeles and maybe also in your town.

"If ye can find a man . . . I will pardon it." Why didn't Abraham keep on pleading with God for Sodom and Gomorrah? He stopped praying after he had asked God to spare the city for ten righteous men. God would have saved the city for *one* righteous man. He had to get that one man, Lot, out of the city before He could destroy it.

Look at how God speaks of His people—

They were as fed horses in the morning: every one neighed after his neighbour's wife [Jer. 5:8].

What is the big sin in our nation today? It is sexual sin, only we don't call it that. We call it "the new morality." But God still calls adultery sin. In fact He uses sarcasm of the first water: He says, "Every man is neighing like a horse for his neighbor's wife." What a picture of our contemporary culture!

> **As a cage is full of birds, so are their houses full of deceit: therefore they are become great, and waxen rich [Jer. 5:27].**

In our generation we have seen a great many kids walk away from their homes because of the conditions which exist in them. I have talked to many of these young people, and I believe this verse gives a valid evaluation of what has happened.

JUDAH REFUSES TO LISTEN

Now Jeremiah concludes his message in chapter 6.

> **For from the least of them even unto the greatest of them every one is given to covetousness; and from the prophet even unto the priest every one dealeth falsely [Jer. 6:13].**

The entire nation was obsessed with covetousness. And covetousness is the great sin in America. There is the coveting of gold and silver, riches, fame, and the neighbor's wife. Those are the things men covet.

> **They have healed also the hurt of the daughter of my people slightly, saying, Peace, peace; when there is no peace [Jer. 6:14].**

There was a reformation on the surface. There was a little healing, but it was like pouring talcum powder on a cancer and then saying it is healed. People were saying "Peace," when there was no peace. And we hear a great deal about peace today, but I think that in reality we are getting ready for the final conflict.

Hear, O earth: behold, I will bring evil upon this people, even the fruit of their thoughts, because they have not hearkened unto my words, nor to my law, but rejected it [Jer. 6:19].

In rejecting the Word of God, they have rejected God. And when men reject God there is always something that follows—

Reprobate silver shall men call them, because the LORD hath rejected them [Jer. 6:30].

Reprobate is actually the same word as *reject*. Therefore, it could read, "Rejected silver shall men call them, because the LORD hath rejected them."

God says to the people of Judah, "You have rejected My law, and I will reject you and when I reject you, the men of the world are going to reject you also." Interesting, isn't it? It worked out that way in Jeremiah's day, and it is working that way in our day. We have spent billions of dollars to buy friends throughout the world; yet we are not loved by this big, bad world because we have rejected God and God will reject us. This is a very solemn message, and we ought not to treat it lightly.

CHAPTERS 7—10

THEME: *Warning delivered in the gate of the Lord's house*

We have seen in chapters 2—6 the prophecies which Jeremiah delivered during the first five years of his ministry. As a young man around twenty years of age, he delivered those severe predictions, condemning his people and pronouncing judgment upon them.

Now the prophecies in chapters 7—10 were given after the Law of the Lord had been discovered in the temple during the time of cleansing ordered by the young king Josiah. Josiah was greatly concerned about his people, which revealed that he had a personal relationship with God as a young man. He and Jeremiah, being approximately the same age and both zealous for God, were probably good friends. Hilkiah the priest, who was evidently the father of Jeremiah, is the one who found the Law of the Lord. The temple was cleaned out and repaired and back in use, which was, of course, a very wonderful thing. Now Jeremiah stands in the gate of the Lord's house and gives a prophecy to his people. This is the way chapter 7 opens—

The word that came to Jeremiah from the LORD, saying,

Stand in the gate of the LORD's house, and proclaim there this word, and say, Hear the word of the LORD, all ye of Judah, that enter in at these gates to worship the LORD [Jer. 7:1–2].

"Stand in the gate of the LORD's house." There are some who think this is very similar to the prophecy that is found in chapter 26 of Jeremiah. The prophecy is similar, but you will notice that it was delivered in the *court* of the house of the Lord—he was no longer standing by the gate but had gone into the court—and it was given during the reign of another king. However, the message is very much the same; Jeremiah had not changed his viewpoint.

Now that the temple has been repaired and the Book of the Law has been found, the people are returning to the temple in droves. Coming back to the temple is the popular thing to do, and they are talking about returning to God. Young Jeremiah hears the conversation of the people, and he gives the following message—

PLEA TO AMEND THEIR WAYS

Thus saith the LORD of hosts, the God of Israel, Amend your ways and your doings, and I will cause you to dwell in this place [Jer. 7:3].

It is evident that, although they are going to the temple and are returning to temple worship, there is no real change in their lives. They are still living as they did when they were worshiping idols. It is only an outward revival at this time. The time would come when it was more real, but at this point it is only a surface movement.

Now we see the attitude of the people, which was the thing that concerns Jeremiah.

Trust ye not in lying words, saying, The temple of the LORD, The temple of the LORD, The temple of the LORD, are these [Jer. 7:4].

You can imagine how the people felt about all of this. They were exclaiming, "My, look at the temple! Isn't it beautiful? Didn't they do a good job of repairing it? Isn't it nice to get back to the temple; it's just like old times!" You see, there was enthusiasm about the temple, but there was no genuine turning to God. This is the thing that Jeremiah noticed. So he said, "Don't trust these lying words that you're saying. You act as if it is the greatest thing in the world just to return to the temple."

If you will turn back to 2 Chronicles and read chapters 34 and 35, it will be very helpful for you to understand what is going on at this time in history. What happened was truly wonderful. Hilkiah gave the Book of the Law to Shaphan, who read it before the king. The king gathered together all the elders of Judah and Jerusalem, and they had the Law read to all the people. Then they made a covenant with God to walk before Him. They celebrated a Passover in Jerusalem: "And there was no passover like to that kept in Israel from the days of Samuel the prophet; neither did all the kings of Israel keep such a passover as Josiah kept, and the priests, and the Levites, and all Judah and Israel that were present, and the inhabitants of Jerusalem. In the eighteenth year of the reign of Josiah was this passover kept" (2 Chron. 35:18–19). They reinstituted the services in the temple with all the sacrifices and feasts. That was good and wonderful. Then what was the problem? The problem was that they were not changing their ways. They lived just as they had lived before. He refers not to the Ten Commandments but to that which the Lord gave them after the Ten Commandments, instructions in Exodus 21—23, which dealt with everyday life in Israel and their relationships to one another.

> **Will ye steal, murder, and commit adultery, and swear falsely, and burn incense unto Baal, and walk after other gods whom ye know not;**
>
> **And come and stand before me in this house, which is called by my name, and say, We are delivered to do all these abominations? [Jer. 7:9–10].**

Although the people were talking about how wonderful the temple was, they were still worshiping Baal. Their philosophy was that, since the temple was repaired and they were at least tipping their hat to God on the Sabbath Day, He would protect them. Now it is true that when people genuinely turn to God, He will protect them, but they were resting on a fact that did not apply to them. They had taken up quite an offering for the rebuilding of the temple, and people who had given generously felt this was all that was necessary for God's blessing.

I know of no book that fits into the present hour with a message for us better than this Book of Jeremiah. After World War II there was a little wave of revival. There were several evangelists out at that time, and the crowds came. During that time I began my Bible studies which were said to have the largest attendance of any midweek service in America. During that time we would hear pastors say that church attendance had doubled and tripled. They were putting chairs in the aisles and building new buildings. Churches were moving out to the suburbs. One pastor I know built a very wonderful church out in suburbia, and he was packing them in—two thousand people in a service. He said, "The trouble was that when I got a new church, I didn't get new people. The same people should have been made new, but they were not." It was the same old people in a new church. They mistook growth in numbers for spiritual growth and development. This is the point that Jeremiah is making.

Now Jeremiah says something further. In fact, our Lord quoted him in His day—

Is this house, which is called by my name, become a den of robbers in your eyes? Behold, even I have seen it, saith the LORD [Jer. 7:11].

This is the same charge that the Lord Jesus used when He cleansed the temple centuries later. In the days of Jeremiah he called it a den of robbers because the people were spending the week robbing their brethren and then would piously come to the temple. There was no change in their business habits or in their relationship with one another.

People today still think there is something valuable in great religious splurges and conventions. This type of thing doesn't appeal to me, because I am not an organization man, nor am I a joiner. I have never enjoyed organizations and conventions. Some people love them. The problem is that some people mistake enthusiasm for a moving of the spirit of God. Now I will probably be as unpopular as Jeremiah when I say that kind of thing is not revival. Nothing is true revival unless it transforms lives.

The Wesleyan movement in England changed lives. It just about put the liquor industry out of business in England. It changed conditions in factories and resulted in the enactment of child labor laws. It was a spiritual movement that reached into the lives of the people. I want to see a spiritual movement today that will reach into the ghetto. When the government reaches into the ghetto with so-called social reform as we have it today, there is crookedness and misappropriation of funds, and nothing is made right. What we need is true revival, which is the only thing that will really change the ghetto.

That was the message of Jeremiah in his day. You can see how popular that young man would have been as he stood there in the gates of the temple and delivered God's message. I can picture him there—a lonely fellow, heartbroken at the message he is giving to his people. But he is giving it faithfully, and it does bring partial revival.

JUDGMENT FOR IDOLATRY

Therefore pray not thou for this people, neither lift up cry nor prayer for them, neither make intercession to me: for I will not hear thee [Jer. 7:16].

God says, "Jeremiah, you don't need to pray for these people until they turn to Me." This is an awesome verse. God says that it is no longer useful to pray for the people. The nation has gone too far away from God. Unless they will turn to God, there is no hope for them.

I believe there are times when we do not need to pray for folk to be blessed. I visited a member of my church in the hospital and prayed for him, then a man in the other bed asked me to pray for him. I asked him whether he was a Christian, and he said he believed in God. I told him that didn't make him a Christian, and then I explained the gospel to him and asked him to put his trust in the Lord Jesus Christ. He said he could not accept that, but he wanted me to pray for him. I told him, "Brother, I will pray for you, but not the way you want me to pray for you. You want me to pray that you will get well and that God will bless you. I am going to pray that you will be *saved*—that is the only prayer I can pray for you." I believe we do too much praying for people to be blessed of God when we ought to be praying that those people will be saved.

This is what God is saying to Jeremiah. "Don't stand there in the temple and pray that these people will not go into captivity. Pray that they will turn back to Me. You are giving them My message, and that is the important thing to do." This gets right down to the nitty-gritty, doesn't it? God is not as interested in your ritual on Sunday as He is in your behavior on Monday. The place to judge whether a Christian is genuine or not is not to watch him in church on Sunday but to see him at work on Monday.

> **But this thing commanded I them, saying, Obey my voice, and I will be your God, and ye shall be my people: and walk ye in all the ways that I have commanded you, that it may be well unto you [Jer. 7:23].**

God clearly states for them again that what He wants is their obedience. Coming to the temple is wonderful, but it is no substitute for obedience.

It has been said that some people go to church to eye the clothes and others go to close their eyes. That may be true in a great number of cases. Their purpose is not really to worship God. Their lives have not been changed. They still gossip, still crucify other Christians behind their backs, still live their lives out in the world—just as Jeremiah's people were still going to the altar of Baal—living without a testimony for the Lord. There is a certain testimony given by going to church, but it is the testimony you give out in the world that counts. This is very real and very personal, isn't it?

> **Yet they hearkened not unto me, nor inclined their ear, but hardened their neck: they did worse than their fathers.**
>
> **Therefore thou shalt speak all these words unto them; but they will not hearken to thee: thou shalt also call unto them; but they will not answer thee [Jer. 7:26–27].**

Jeremiah did not have people come forward and declare themselves for God. His message went unheeded; yet it was his responsibility to deliver the message. God told him to do the job, to give out His Word, even if there was no response to it. It is not important for us to be able to count noses and see a response to our message. The important thing is the report we must give to God, to be faithful in giving out His Word and backing it up with our lives.

> **Cut off thine hair, O Jerusalem, and cast it away, and take up a lamentation on high places; for the LORD hath rejected and forsaken the generation of his wrath [Jer. 7:29].**

God calls them "the generation of his wrath." Judgment will come to Jerusalem.

> **And they have built the high places of Tophet, which is in the valley of the son of Hinnom, to burn their sons and their daughters in the fire; which I commanded them not, neither came it into my heart [Jer. 7:31].**

"Tophet" was the high place of the valley of Hinnom, where the children were sacrificed upon the heated brass arms of Moloch.

NO ONE REPENTED OF HIS WICKEDNESS

Chapter 8 continues Jeremiah's message as he stands in the gate of the Lord's house.

> **The wise men are ashamed, they are dismayed and taken: lo, they have rejected the word of the LORD; and what wisdom is in them? [Jer. 8:9].**

Their crowning sin is that they are rejecting the Word of the Lord.

This is the crowning sin of America also. The prevailing feeling is that if our economy is all right, we are all right. However, many folk are beginning to realize that the economy can be all right and we can be all wrong.

After World War II we hastened to get the atom bomb into our arsenal of weapons. Of course we need to protect ourselves, but we forgot that any nation, any church, or any individual disintegrates from the *inside*. It is not what happens on the outside, but what happens on the inside that is the crucial issue.

Jeremiah enters deeply into the feelings of his people, sharing with them this wail—

> **The harvest is past, the summer is ended, and we are not saved.**
>
> **For the hurt of the daughter of my people am I hurt; I am black; astonishment hath taken hold on me.**
>
> **Is there no balm in Gilead; is there no physician there? why then is not the health of the daughter of my people recovered? [Jer. 8:20–22].**

Although God had made adequate provision for their restoration, they refuse the remedy.

JEREMIAH SHARES GOD'S HEARTBREAK

Chapter 9 begins with an expression of Jeremiah's personal heartbreak as he sees his people spurn the tender solicitude of God.

> **Oh that my head were waters, and mine eyes a fountain of tears, that I might weep day and night for the slain of the daughter of my people! [Jer. 9:1].**

This is the effect it had on Jeremiah. How did he give his message? Was he a hard-boiled kind of man who liked to criticize others and rule them out? No, he stood there and gave his message with tears streaming down his face. The message that he gave broke his heart.

Centuries later, people of Israel saw Jesus weeping over the city of Jerusalem when He had a harsh message to deliver to that city and were reminded of Jeremiah, the weeping prophet, and some of them even thought Jesus was Jeremiah who had returned to them.

> **Oh that I had in the wilderness a lodging place of wayfaring men; that I might leave my people, and go from them! for they be all adulterers, and assembly of treacherous men [Jer. 9:2].**

He longed to get away into a wilderness place where he would not have to see the sin of his people which was bringing his nation to ruin.

> **Thus saith the LORD, Let not the wise man glory in his wisdom, neither let the mighty man glory in his might, let not the rich man glory in his riches:**
>
> **But let him that glorieth glory in this, that he understandeth and knoweth me, that I am the LORD which exercise lovingkindness, judgment, and righteousness, in the earth: for in these things I delight, saith the LORD [Jer. 9:23–24].**

These are two wonderful verses of Scripture. They can stand alone and are often quoted alone. However, we need to remember that they were spoken to a people who had rejected the Word of God.

As a nation, what are the things we glory in? Obviously, we trust in human wisdom, in riches, and in power. We need to be reminded that our strength is not in the brain trust in Washington. Our strength is not in Wall Street, the stock market, and the economy. Our strength does not lie in the cleverness of politicians. Our strength is not found in the fact that we have nuclear weapons. Any strength that we have must lie in our spiritual values, our moral values, our character, and our purpose. And these things are not even taught in our schools and colleges today. We have brought forth a generation that is rude, a generation that has no sense of moral purpose. In fact, we have lost our way—as Jeremiah said to his people—on the dark mountains. In our day America is just coasting along; and, when you start coasting, you are going downhill.

I know it is not popular to say these things. I am afraid I am not making friends and influencing people—but neither did Jeremiah. I am going to stand with him, because I believe there is still hope for revival in our land.

"Let him that glorieth glory in this, that he understandeth and knoweth me." What we need desperately is a group of leaders who know something other than the present godless philosophy. We need people who know God, who know His Word and are obeying it. The great need in this country today is a return to God. We need to set aside our hypocrisy and our sophistication and our illusion that we are such a smart people. We brag about our achievements when our great need is to walk in a way that will glorify God.

Chapter 10 concludes Jeremiah's message in the gate of the Lord's house, and it begins a section (chs. 10—12) of reform and revival after finding the Book of the Law.

The finding of the Book of the Law had a tremendous effect on King Josiah. He realized how far the people had fallen from God's intention for them. It moved that man, and he was tremendously changed. He brought his people into a covenant with God that they would serve Him.

THE FOOLISHNESS OF IDOLATRY

In this chapter we see that the people were substituting something for God. People have always had substitutes for God. Anyone who is not worshiping the true and living God has some substitute for Him. It may be that the person himself becomes his god—there are a great number of people who actually worship themselves. Others worship money and are willing to be dishonest to become rich. Others worship fame and will sell their honor in order to obtain some unworthy goal. There are many substitutes for God, and Jeremiah talks about this:

> **Hear ye the word which the LORD speaketh unto you, O house of Israel:**
>
> **Thus saith the LORD, Learn not the way of the heathen, and be not dismayed at the signs of heaven; for the heathen are dismayed at them [Jer. 10:1–2].**

People today are still doing what they did in the time of Jeremiah, trying to regulate their lives by the zodiac. They want to know what sign they were born under and all that nonsense. It is given out through our news media as though it were genuine!

God warns, "Learn not the way of the heathen." My friend, the astrology that is being promoted today is something which has been picked up from the pagan world.

> **For the customs of the people are vain: for one cutteth a tree out of the forest, the work of the hands of the workman, with the axe.**
>
> **They deck it with silver and with gold; they fasten it with nails and with hammers, that it move not [Jer. 10:3–4].**

There are some folk who interpret Jeremiah's denunciation of idolatry to be a condemnation of the modern Christmas tree. That is utterly preposterous and ridiculous. Jeremiah is not talking about Christmas trees—nobody in his day had a Christmas tree! He is talking to his people about worshiping idols.

"The customs of the people are vain"—they are empty. Obviously Jeremiah is talking about idolatry. He is ridiculing with bitter irony the idolatry of his day. He reminds them that they go out to the woods, cut down a tree, shape it into an image, deck it with silver and gold, fasten it with nails—and that's their god! It is like worshiping a scarecrow! Now, my friend, if at Christmas time you fall on your knees before your Christmas tree and worship it, Jeremiah's warning could have reference to you. But I don't know of even an unsaved pagan in the country who *worships* a Christmas tree. They use it as a decoration, then throw it out with the trash when Christmas is over. Rather than worshiping a Christmas tree, the danger I see is the worship of self at Christmastime—*getting* everything possible for self.

> **Forasmuch as there is none like unto thee, O Lord; thou art great, and thy name is great in might [Jer. 10:6].**

The Lord cannot be compared to anything. How ridiculous it is to turn from the true and living God to worship the things around you and get your leading from the zodiac!

> **Thus shall ye say unto them, The gods that have not made the heavens and the earth, even they shall perish from the earth, and from under these heavens [Jer. 10:11].**

The gods of the heathen did not create the universe. Our God, the living God, created it.

> **He hath made the earth by his power, he hath established the world by his wisdom, and hath stretched out the heavens by his discretion [Jer. 10:12].**

The stars are up there in their places because *God* put them there. He placed them where *He* wanted them. He didn't ask you or me how we wanted them arranged. This is *His* universe, and He is the only One who is worthy of our worship. We may smile at the people of previous centuries who cut down a tree to make a god. We call ourselves intelligent and civilized; yet our people spend millions of dollars to try to discern their future by the zodiac, going to fortune-tellers and palm readers and all that sort of thing. If people today are so intelligent, why don't they worship the living and true God and get into reality?

O Lord, I know that the way of man is not in himself: it is not in man that walketh to direct his steps [Jer. 10:23].

No man can walk aright apart from the revelation of God in His Word. The minute a man turns from the Word of God, he is on a detour. That is our natural course. In fact, we begin that way. I used to take my little grandson for a walk around the block when he was learning to walk. He was a wonderful little fellow, but he wore me out because he wanted to walk up the sidewalk of every house we passed; and when we came to a driveway, he would want to run out in the street, and when we would get to a corner he would want to go the wrong way. I have never seen a little fellow who wanted to go in as many wrong ways as he did. One day when we finally got home, I said to him, "Kim, you're just like your grandfather. When he gets away from the Word of God, he always goes down a detour." My friend, "it is not in man . . . to direct his steps." We are dependent upon the omniscient God for direction in every area of our lives.

CHAPTERS 11—13

THEME: *Israel disobeyed God's covenant made in the wilderness*

In chapters 11 and 12 Jeremiah delivers this tremendous message after the Law has been read to the people. I must remind you that following the giving of the Ten Commandments in Exodus 20, God went on to pronounce certain judgments if the Law were disobeyed. These are the things that Jeremiah emphasizes, the aspects of the Law which condition the way we live our lives—the way you treat your neighbor, the way you conduct your business, and the kind of social life you are living. Are you one of these church members who is actually worshiping sex? I know men who have left their wives to marry some little girl who didn't have anything upstairs but had a whole lot downstairs, and they think they can still serve the Lord! Jeremiah makes it clear that if you have done that, you've gone down a detour and are far away from God.

Many people talk about being fundamental and correct in their doctrine (I hope you understand that I insist upon that), but what is equally important is the kind of life that you are living. How *honest* are you? How *clean* are you in your living? That is what Jeremiah is insisting upon here. Most of us, if we were honest, would get down before God and confess our need to walk with Him, to be close to Him. But the people didn't do it in Jeremiah's day, and there won't be many who do it in our day either.

The word that came to Jeremiah from the LORD, saying,

Hear ye the words of this covenant, and speak unto the men of Judah, and to the inhabitants of Jerusalem [Jer. 11:1–2].

"This covenant"—When the Law was found and read to the people, King Josiah called in the leaders and they made an oath that they were going to follow the Word of God.

And say thou unto them, Thus saith the LORD God of Israel; Cursed be the man that obeyeth not the words of this covenant [Jer. 11:3].

Before they found the Book of the Law, the people did not know the Law. Now they know it and their responsibility is great: God says, "Cursed be the man that obeyeth not the words of this covenant."

I have said many times that I would rather be a heathen in some dark corner of the earth bowing down before an idol, than to be a member of a church where the pastor faithfully preaches the Word of God and to have done nothing in response to it. May I say, I have more respect for that heathen man, and God may yet bring the gospel to him. But that church member who has heard the gospel and rejected it—God will certainly judge him.

Now this chapter closes with the fact that Jeremiah is actually rejected by his hometown, Anathoth.

But I was like a lamb or an ox that is brought to the slaughter; and I knew not that they had devised devices against me, saying, Let us destroy the tree with the fruit thereof, and let us cut him off from the land of the living, that his name may be no more remembered.

But, O LORD of hosts, that judgest righteously, that triest the reins and the heart, let me see thy vengeance on them: for unto thee have I revealed my cause.

Therefore thus saith the LORD of the men of Anathoth, that seek thy life, saying, Prophesy not in the name of the LORD, that thou die not by our hand [Jer. 11:19–21].

God tells Jeremiah, "There is no use speaking to Anathoth anymore. They have rejected Me, and they want to kill you. Don't bother to prophesy to them any longer."

There are churches today who no longer stand for the things of God or teach the Word of God as they once did. And some people think it is terrible that their memberships are dwindling and that the churches are being deserted. What *is* terrible is that the Word of God is not being taught in their pulpits. Jeremiah stopped giving the Word of God in Anathoth. He went somewhere else, because the people were going to kill him; they had rejected the Word of God.

What a picture we have here! It *cost* this man Jeremiah something to stand for God. It broke his own heart and alienated his hometown from him. In John 4:44 we read, ". . . Jesus himself testified, that a prophet hath no honour in his own country." Our Lord had to leave His hometown of Nazareth and move His headquarters to Capernaum. That is what young Jeremiah had to do also.

Jeremiah is delivering a message to these people unlike any we hear today. Today we say, "Come to Jesus, and He will give you a new personality, and He may even make you rich. You're going to get along real well." That's not what we learn from Jeremiah and his life. Jeremiah says that it will cost you something to turn to God—but it will be worth everything you have to pay.

In spite of the fact that Judah made a covenant to serve God, the revival in the land proved to be a largely surface movement. There is no question that the words of Jeremiah had their effect and that there were some who in genuineness turned to the Lord. Jeremiah had preached, "Then the LORD said unto me, Proclaim all these words in the cities of Judah, and in the streets of Jerusalem, saying, Hear ye the words of this covenant, and do them" (v. 6).

However, things in the nation were deteriorating. After the revival, interest in spiritual things began to wear off, and the people returned to their old ways. Even King Josiah made a grave blunder. He went out to battle against the king of Egypt, Pharaoh-nechoh, and they fought at Megiddo. Josiah was fatally wounded, and Jeremiah mourned for him: "And Jeremiah lamented for Josiah: and all the singing men and the singing women spake of Josiah in their lamentations to this day, and made them an ordinance in Israel: and, behold, they are written in the lamentations" (2 Chron. 35:25).

Jeremiah wept because he knew that the people not only would return to idolatry but they would sink even farther into immorality. And, of course, they did. Jeremiah had to give the people a message that they didn't want to hear. They rejected his message and were plotting to kill him, so that he had to leave his hometown of Anathoth. Had Josiah still been alive, he would have protected Jeremiah, but Josiah was gone now.

Jehoahaz came to the throne but reigned for only three months. Pharaoh-nechoh then raised Jehoiakim to the throne of Judah. Jehoiakim had to pay a tax to Egypt, so he taxed the land heavily. It wasn't very long until Nebuchadnezzar defeated the Egyptian king and Jehoiakim became a vassal of Babylon. This lasted for three years, and then Jehoiakim rebelled against the king of Babylon, ignoring Jeremiah's warning not to do so. Jeremiah had also warned earlier against the alliance with Egypt as a source of false confidence, but the kings of Judah paid no attention to him and continually became more corrupt.

JEREMIAH'S QUESTION

As we come to chapter 12 we have entered a very evil period in the life of the nation, and the only light remaining is this man Jeremiah. Josiah has been slain, Jeremiah has been forced to leave his hometown, and evil men have come to the throne. Conditions seem only to get worse. At this point Jeremiah—and I believe every honest Christian—has doubts come into his heart. Dark thoughts come into his mind, and he wonders why God permits certain things. Every pastor who has ever stood for the things of God at times wonders why God does not move. He looks around and sees that it is his very best people who are suffering; the most spiritual folk seem to be having more trouble than anyone else. We all wonder why God permits this. Even David questioned God when he saw ". . . the wicked in great power, and spreading himself like a green bay tree" (Ps. 37:35). Listen now to Jeremiah as he talks to the Lord:

> **Righteous art thou, O Lord, when I plead with thee: yet let me talk with thee of thy judgments: Wherefore doth the way of the wicked prosper? wherefore are all they happy that deal very treacherously?**

> **Thou hast planted them, yea, they have taken root: they grow, yea, they bring forth fruit: thou art near in their mouth, and far from their reins [Jer. 12:1–2].**

"Oh, they talk about You, Lord, but they're far from You, and they prosper. Why do You permit that?" That was Jeremiah's question. That's my question too. I'd like to ask God that today: "Lord, why do You permit it?" I don't have the answer, and I don't think Jeremiah or David ever had the answer either. God allows the wicked to prosper, and we see them spreading themselves like a green bay tree. Why doesn't God prosper those who are really interested in supporting fine Christian missionaries? I've asked Him that, and I don't have the answer.

> **But thou, O LORD, knowest me: thou hast seen me, and tried mine heart toward thee: pull them out like sheep for the slaughter, and prepare them for the day of slaughter [Jer. 12:3].**

Jeremiah says, "Why don't You judge them? They are the ones who should be judged."

> **How long shall the land mourn, and the herbs of every field wither, for the wickedness of them that dwell therein? the beasts are consumed, and the birds; because they said, He shall not see our last end [Jer. 12:4].**

"How long shall the land mourn"—in other words, "Lord, why don't You move?" God's answer to Jeremiah and to you and me today is one that we must accept—it's the best we have. God says, "I know what I'm doing. You *trust* Me, rest in Me." Remember Jeremiah began this passage, "*Righteous* art thou, O LORD." My friend, what God is doing today—however peculiar it may seem to us—is *right,* and we will be able to see and understand that someday. That is where faith must enter in. We walk by faith and not by sight.

Jeremiah alone stands for God. Jehoiakim, a corrupt ruler, is on the throne. Things are getting worse, and he wonders what is going to happen. God has already assured Jeremiah that He will take care of the situation. In chapter 11 verse 16 "The LORD called thy name, A green olive tree, fair, and of goodly fruit: with the noise of a great tumult he hath kindled fire upon it, and the branches of it are broken." Paul refers to this in Romans 11 saying that the good olive tree has been cut off and set aside. That is exactly what God did to these people. And today, out of that same root, He's bringing forth a wild olive tree. That is you and me: the church has been grafted into that root which is Christ. He is the ". . . root out of a dry ground . . ." (Isa. 53:2), and He brings life. God says to Jeremiah, "I'll take care of this. I'll be the One who will deal with this." God has a plan which extends far beyond the circumstances that Jeremiah could see.

> **If thou hast run with the footmen, and they have wearied thee, then how canst thou contend with horses? and if in the land of peace, wherein thou trustedst, they wearied thee, then how wilt thou do in the swelling of Jordan? [Jer. 12:5].**

You'll forgive me, I'm not trying to be irreverent, but this is actually what God is saying to Jeremiah: "If you are troubled now by what things are going to happen, well, you ain't seen nothing yet! Things are to get lots worse, Jeremiah. And if you're troubled now, what are you going to do when it really gets bad?"

Friend, things may look bad to us today, but they are going to get worse. I hope the knowledge of that will help draw you closer to God. He does not explain all the details to us as we might wish He would, but He does tell us that we can trust Him to always do the right thing.

> **Mine heritage is unto me as a speckled bird, the birds round about are against her; come ye, assemble all the beasts of the field, come to devour [Jer. 12:9].**

Don't tell me God doesn't have a sense of humor. He says here, "Jeremiah, you're a speckled bird!" You see, every crow thinks his little offspring is blacker than any other crow, but when an egg hatches and it's speckled, that tells you something. And Jeremiah was a speckled bird. The people said to him, "We thought you were for us, that you were one of us. But you're not, you're speckled." Well, my friend, I'm a speckled bird too, and I have a notion you might be one. If you're standing for God, you *are* a speckled bird! God says, "Jeremiah, you might as well accept it: you're a speckled bird, if you stand with Me."

And it shall come to pass, after that I have plucked them out I will return, and have compassion on them, and will bring them again, every man to his heritage, and every man to his land [Jer. 12:15].

Why is it that the rich are prospering? God says, "Jeremiah, I'll take care of that. And I'll tell you what is going to happen: They are going into captivity. But I have remembered the land, and I'm going to bring them back into the land."

PARABLE IN ACTION—THE LINEN GIRDLE

Chapter 13 is another great chapter. I think it is interesting because, even when conditions are so terribly serious, you just can't help but smile. God is giving a parable to Judah, and it is the parable of the girdle!

Thus saith the LORD unto me, Go and get thee a linen girdle, and put it upon thy loins, and put it not in water [Jer. 13:1].

I just can't help but smile at this. I don't think that Jeremiah was putting on weight. In fact, I would think he had been losing weight. God told him to get a girdle and wear it. But it wasn't because he was getting fat—a girdle wasn't worn for that purpose in that day. You see, today a girdle is used to try to achieve an hourglass figure when it is more like a barrel! In that day a girdle was something worn to bind up the flowing garments to ready oneself for service.

The girdle is a sign of service. The Lord Jesus spoke of His servants having their ". . . loins . . . girded about . . ." (Luke 12:35). That is, they are to be ready for service. You remember that He girded Himself with a linen cloth and began to wash the disciples' feet. This had a twofold meaning: *He*, the great Servant, was preparing *them* for service by washing their feet so they could have fellowship with Him. For if you don't have fellowship with Him, you can't serve. Service is fellowship with Christ. It is not teaching a Sunday school class, singing a solo, or preaching a sermon. Service is fellowship with Christ. It is being cleansed and used for what He wants to do. God doesn't use dirty cups or dirty vessels.

Now Jeremiah is told to do something very interesting with this girdle:

> **And the word of the LORD came unto me the second time, saying,**
>
> **Take the girdle that thou hast got, which is upon thy loins, and arise, go to Euphrates, and hide it there in a hole of the rock.**
>
> **So I went, and hid it by Euphrates, as the LORD commanded me [Jer. 13:3–5].**

There has always been a lot of debate as to whether Jeremiah actually went down to the Euphrates and hid the girdle. I think he did. There was traffic in the day going to and fro between nations, and I think Jeremiah actually made this trip. He did this very strange thing, and when he came back, people probably said, "Where have you been, Jeremiah?" He would reply, "I've been down to Babylon." "What have you been doing down there? Did you go as a representative of the king, or did you go down there on a business trip?" Jeremiah would have to answer, "No, I went down there to hide a girdle!" Now, my friend, I think the crowd laughed at that.

> **And it came to pass after many days, that the LORD said unto me, Arise, go to Euphrates, and take the girdle from thence, which I commanded thee to hide there.**

> Then I went to Euphrates, and digged, and took the gir-
> dle from the place where I had hid it: and, behold, the
> girdle was marred, it was profitable for nothing [Jer.
> 13:6–7].

Jeremiah was to wear the girdle and not wash it but let it get dirtier
and dirtier. I think it finally got so dirty that he couldn't bear to wear it
anymore. Then God told him to bury it in Babylon as an object lesson.
When he returned and dug it up, he found "it was profitable for nothing." What does this strange action mean?

> Then the word of the LORD came unto me, saying,

> Thus saith the LORD, After this manner will I mar the
> pride of Judah, and the great pride of Jerusalem [Jer.
> 13:8–9].

God is saying that because the people of Judah are continually sinking
into iniquity they will reach the place where there is no hope for them.
He is going to send them into Babylonian captivity. The object lesson
was impressive. God uses some very funny things to teach His people.

> Give glory to the LORD your God, before he cause dark-
> ness, and before your feet stumble upon the dark moun-
> tains, and, while ye look for light, he turn it into the
> shadow of death, and make it gross darkness [Jer.
> 13:16].

God says to His people, "It's getting nighttime now. It's going to be
dark, and you won't know where to go because you are lost in the
mountains." Yet He still asks them to turn to Him.

> The cities of the south shall be shut up, and none shall
> open them: Judah shall be carried away captive all of it,
> it shall be wholly carried away captive [Jer. 13:19].

God tells them exactly what is going to happen. He makes it very clear what He will do.

> **Can the Ethiopian change his skin, or the leopard his spots? then may ye also do good, that are accustomed to do evil [Jer. 13:23].**

It is impossible for an unsaved person to do good. All of the do-gooders are not really pleasing God. Until a man does his work in the name of the Lord Jesus Christ and for His glory and honor, he is simply doing the work for himself for selfish reasons. No genuine goodness can come out of an evil heart.

CHAPTERS 14 AND 15

THEME: Backsliding nation judged by drought and famine

Up to this point Jeremiah has been prophesying during the reign of Josiah. Now we find him delivering a prophecy during the reign of Jehoiakim. King Josiah during the last part of his reign did a very foolish thing. He fought against Nechoh, a pharaoh of Egypt, and there at Megiddo Josiah was killed. Jeremiah mourned for him; he had been his friend. After the death of Josiah, the nation began to drop back into idolatry; in fact, its plunge downward was swift and terrible, as we shall see in this section.

DROUGHT

God's first warning to the nation was drought.

> **The word of the Lord that came to Jeremiah concerning the dearth.**

> **Judah mourneth, and the gates thereof languish; they are black unto the ground; and the cry of Jerusalem is gone up [Jer. 14:1–2].**

The drought was apparently a very severe one. There had been a drought during the reign of Ahab, and at that time Elijah was the messenger from God. Now there is a drought, and Jeremiah is the messenger to the southern kingdom of Judah.

> **Because the ground is chapt, for there was no rain in the earth, the plowmen were ashamed, they covered their heads [Jer. 14:4].**

The ground is barren and cracked for want of rainfall.

> **Yea, the hind also calved in the field, and forsook it,
> because there was no grass [Jer. 14:5].**

Even the deer would leave their offspring because there was no water to drink and no grazing land. It would mean death to the calf and to the mother also. All of this revealed the fact that God was judging them. This is one of the thirteen famines mentioned in Scripture, and all of them were judgments of God upon the land. Just as the land was barren and unfruitful, so were the lives of the people because they had rejected the water of life. God was showing them that what was happening to the physical earth was also happening in a spiritual sense to their hearts.

Jeremiah goes to God to confess the sins of the people.

> **O LORD, though our iniquities testify against us, do thou
> it for thy name's sake: for our backslidings are many;
> we have sinned against thee [Jer. 14:7].**

Notice that Jeremiah takes his place with his people as being one of the sinners. There is no boasting here. He does not show any signs of a critical attitude toward the people. He says, "We have backslidden, and *we* have sinned." It is so easy for God's people to be critical of others. They pray almost like the Pharisee whom our Lord Jesus told us about in Luke 18:11–12. "I thank You, Lord, that I am so good. I am a separated Christian and I do this and I don't do that. I am a nice, sweet Sunday school Christian. Now Mr. So-and-So over there is a dirty old man, and Mrs. So-and-So never does anything for You, and Miss So-and-So is a real gossip." That is not identifying oneself with the people of God! You will notice that Jeremiah didn't pray that kind of a prayer. He identified himself with God's sinning people and said, "We have backslidden, and we have sinned." My friend, if you can take your place before God, confessing your own sins as well as the sins of your people, then you can speak to them about the judgment of God. But until you can do that, you shouldn't try to speak on God's behalf.

As we move on through this chapter, we see that the darkness has gathered, and the people are stumbling on the dark mountains.

> **Then said I, Ah, Lord God! behold, the prophets say unto them, Ye shall not see the sword, neither shall ye have famine; but I will give you assured peace in this place [Jer. 14:13].**

The false prophets were predicting peace and prosperity—everything was going to be wonderful.

> **Then the Lord said unto me, The prophets prophesy lies in my name: I sent them not, neither have I commanded them, neither spake unto them: they prophesy unto you a false vision and divination, and a thing of nought, and the deceit of their heart [Jer. 14:14].**

You see, Jeremiah is very much alone now that King Josiah is dead. And he is wondering—*Am I giving the correct message, or are the other prophets right?* He is not quite sure; so he goes to God about it. God reassures him, "I want you to know that the false prophets are lying. I didn't send them. You are the one giving My message." You can see that this will put Jeremiah right back on the firing line.

> **Therefore thou shalt say this word unto them; Let mine eyes run down with tears night and day, and let them not cease: for the virgin daughter of my people is broken with a great breach, with a very grievous blow [Jer. 14:17].**

The message was breaking the heart of Jeremiah. He was weeping as he gave the message to his people. God wanted the people to know that *His* heart was breaking. Jeremiah was not only giving the message from God, but he was expressing the feelings of God as well.

We all need to realize that we are witnesses for God. If you are a child of God, you are a witness for God, and you are saying something by your life. We need to be very careful when we speak the Word of God that our lives conform to it. We are not to be giving out the Word in a coldhearted manner. There must be feeling in it. If there is not, then there is something radically wrong with us.

INEVITABLE JUDGMENT

In chapter 15 we see that Jeremiah is a brokenhearted man who wants to go to God to pray for his people. That was very right and fine. However, God has something interesting to say to him:

> **Then said the LORD unto me, Though Moses and Samuel stood before me, yet my mind could not be toward this people: cast them out of my sight, and let them go forth [Jer. 15:1].**

The people have gone too far, and judgment must come upon them. They have gone over the borderline where there is absolutely no possibility for reprieve. They will not escape captivity. The Lord tells Jeremiah that he shouldn't think that God is not hearing his prayers. There was nothing wrong in Jeremiah's prayers. God says that even if *Moses* stood before Him, He would not listen. You will remember in Exodus 32 that Moses was a marvelous intercessor for the people. When God threatened to destroy the people, Moses had stood before Him as their intercessor. God answered his prayer and spared the people. But now, even if Moses were acting as the intercessor for the people, it wouldn't do any good. Samuel was another who had prayed for the people. Judgment had been averted again and again because of Samuel. But God says that even if *Samuel* were to pray now, there could be no averting of the judgment. The people had stepped across the borderline, and judgment was inevitable.

Now we can understand why Jeremiah is giving a message of nothing but judgment.

> **For who shall have pity upon thee, O Jerusalem? or who shall bemoan thee? or who shall go aside to ask how thou doest?**

> Thou hast forsaken me, saith the Lord, thou art gone
> backward: therefore will I stretch out my hand against
> thee, and destroy thee; I am weary with repenting [Jer.
> 15:5–6].

"Thou art gone backward"—that's backsliding.

"I am weary with repenting." They have come to Him over and
over with their weeping and their promises to do better, but they continually go right back into the same old sin. God is tired of it all, and
He says the time has now come when He intends to judge them.

JEREMIAH'S PERSONAL DISTRESS

You can see that this message would not increase the popularity of
poor Jeremiah. King Josiah was his friend, but not King Jehoiakim.
Jehoiakim was an evil man. Jeremiah was the fly in the ointment for
Jehoiakim. He considered Jeremiah nothing but a troublemaker.

In spite of the fact that Jeremiah is a weeping prophet who must
deliver this very difficult message, he really had a sense of humor. He
went to the Lord and cried out:

> Woe is me, my mother, that thou hast borne me a man of
> strife and a man of contention to the whole earth! I have
> neither lent on usury, nor men have lent to me on usury;
> yet every one of them doth curse me [Jer. 15:10].

Jeremiah says, "Nobody likes me. I don't lend money on interest and I
don't borrow money on interest, yet everyone curses me." We still
have an adage today that says if we want to lose a friend, lend him
money.

I have seen what the lending of money can do to Christian friends.
I remember a man who lent money to his friend who had some project
in mind and thought he could double the money in a hurry. Actually,
he lost all the money and couldn't pay back his friend. That broke up a
good friendship and wrecked their relationship. So if you want to
start losing your friends, lend them money! Jeremiah says, "You'd

think I had been lending money around here—nobody wants to have anything to do with me."

During this difficult time, Jeremiah turns to the Word of God—remember that the Law of the Lord had been found in the Temple and was available to him.

> **Thy words were found, and I did eat them; and thy word was unto me the joy and rejoicing of mine heart: for I am called by thy name, O LORD God of hosts [Jer. 15:16].**

He found his consolation in it. He ate it and he digested it and it became a part of him. Oh, how we need to get into the Word of God today. We don't need just a little surface learning of a few rules, or just a little guideline of a few steps to take. We need to digest it so that it becomes part of our being. It will bring joy and rejoicing to the heart just as it did for Jeremiah. Only the Word of God can do this.

I received a letter from a man who heard our broadcast when I was in Galatians. He heard one word: *Father*. That arrested his attention. May I say to you that God is still using His Word today. Oh, how important the Word of God is!

Jeremiah is in real difficulty. Remember that his hometown rejected him and got rid of him. His own family rejected him. His life is actually in danger.

> **And I will make thee unto this people a fenced brasen wall: and they shall fight against thee, but they shall not prevail against thee: for I am with thee to save thee and to deliver thee, saith the LORD.**
>
> **And I will deliver thee out of the hand of the wicked, and I will redeem thee out of the hand of the terrible [Jer. 15:20–21].**

God says, "You just stay on the firing line, and I will take care of you."

CHAPTERS 16 AND 17

THEME: God forbids Jeremiah to marry

The days are becoming increasingly difficult. The nation of Judah is coming to the end of its rope. As nearly as I can judge, it is within ten years of the destruction of Jerusalem at this particular time.

> **The word of the LORD came also unto me, saying,**
>
> **Thou shalt not take thee a wife, neither shalt thou have sons or daughters in this place.**
>
> **For thus saith the LORD concerning the sons and concerning the daughters that are born in this place, and concerning their mothers that bare them, and concerning their fathers that begat them in this land;**
>
> **They shall die of grievous deaths; they shall not be lamented; neither shall they be buried; but they shall be as dung upon the face of the earth: and they shall be consumed by the sword, and by famine; and their carcases shall be meat for the fowls of heaven, and for the beasts of the earth [Jer. 16:1–4].**

God reveals to Jeremiah the horror that is to come. He tells Jeremiah not to get married, and I think the reason is quite obvious. If you will turn to Psalm 137, which was written after the Babylonian captivity, you will see the fate children suffered. In the last two verses it says that Babylon will be destroyed and they will do to her just *as she had done to Judah:* "O daughter of Babylon, who art to be destroyed; happy shall he be, that rewardeth thee as thou hast served us. Happy shall he be, that taketh and dasheth thy little ones against the stones" (Ps. 137:8–9). When Nebuchadnezzar took the city of Jerusalem, the conquerors seized little children and dashed their heads against the stones! God asked Jeremiah not to get married because He wanted to spare Jeremiah this anguish.

Under certain circumstances it is best not to bring children into this world. I sometimes wonder about the times in which we live. My heart goes out to the little ones today. I look at my own grandchildren and, actually, tears come into my eyes. They may live out their lives through some terrible times, so I pray for them and ask the Lord to protect them. A great deal could be said about this. There is a time when it would be better not to have children.

Here is a bright note—

> **Therefore, behold, the days come, saith the Lord, that it shall no more be said, The Lord liveth, that brought up the children of Israel out of the land of Egypt;**

> **But, the Lord liveth, that brought up the children of Israel from the land of the north, and from all the lands whither he had driven them: and I will bring them again into their land that I gave unto their fathers [Jer. 16:14–15].**

In this dark moment in Judah's history, God let Jeremiah see a brilliant future. It is as if he looks down the dark tunnel of the future and sees the light at the other end. It is interesting that this theme recurs throughout the writings of the prophets. It never got so dark but what the prophets didn't see the light that was coming, and the darker the night was, the brighter the light appeared to be. God says the day is coming when He will bring them back from captivity, back home to their own land.

> **Therefore, behold, I will this once cause them to know, I will cause them to know mine hand and my might; and they shall know that my name is The Lord [Jer. 16:21].**

It is my personal opinion that God is going to have to teach my country that He is the Lord. I get the impression that America doesn't know

God is out there. When He does make Himself known, I am afraid it will be very impressive.

MESSAGE OF THE UNMARRIED PROPHET

The sin of Judah is written with a pen of iron, and with the point of a diamond: it is graven upon the table of their heart, and upon the horns of your altars;

Whilst their children remember their altars and their groves by the green trees upon the high hills [Jer. 17:1–2].

There was evil in everything they did. It even permeated their religion.

Thus saith the LORD; Cursed be the man that trusteth in man, and maketh flesh his arm, and whose heart departeth from the LORD [Jer. 17:5].

It might be well for us to put that up as a motto today. Sometimes we think we can depend on certain men or on certain political parties to work out the problems of the world. You and I are cursed people if we put our trust in men and what men can do. This is the day to trust God.

Blessed is the man that trusteth in the LORD, and whose hope the LORD is [Jer. 17:7].

We shall be blessed if we trust Him.

For he shall be as a tree planted by the waters, and that spreadeth out her roots by the river, and shall not see when heat cometh, but her leaf shall be green; and shall not be careful in the year of drought, neither shall cease from yielding fruit [Jer. 17:8].

This is the same thought that we find in the first psalm: Blessed is the man whose ". . . delight is in the law of the LORD; and in his law doth he meditate day and night. And he shall be like a tree planted by the rivers of water, that bringeth forth his fruit in his season; his leaf also shall not wither; and whatsoever he doeth shall prosper" (Ps. 1:2–3).

> **The heart is deceitful above all things, and desperately wicked: who can know it? [Jer. 17:9].**

This is true of your heart and my heart. Unfortunately, we all have heart trouble.

> **I the LORD search the heart, I try the reins, even to give every man according to his ways, and according to the fruit of his doings [Jer. 17:10].**

Only God can make a heart transplant. Man is now doing that sort of thing in the physical sense, but God has been doing it in the spiritual sense for a long time. When we come to Him, He gives us new life—we are born anew and given a new nature. Sometimes we who are ministers use the expression, "Give your heart to the Lord." Well, what would God want with that old, dirty, filthy heart of yours or mine? He doesn't want it. The heart is deceitful. He wants to give you a new heart. He is a heart specialist; He is the Great Physician.

Now we will conclude this chapter with a great verse:

> **A glorious high throne from the beginning is the place of our sanctuary [Jer. 17:12].**

This is the hope of man. All men have hearts which are deceitful, dirty, filthy, and wicked. But there is a sanctuary. "A glorious high throne from the beginning is the place of our sanctuary." A sanctuary is not only a place of worship; it is a place of safety, a place of peace. God gave to His people certain cities which were to be cities of refuge, sanctuaries where they would be protected.

My friend, these are difficult days. It is dangerous to walk the streets of our cities. Even in our homes we are not safe from a bomb that may come from the other side of the world. Where can we go to be safe? There is a sanctuary, and it is the high throne of our God. That is the place where you and I can go. And He *asks* us to come. "Having therefore, brethren, boldness to enter into the holiest by the blood of Jesus, By a new and living way, which he hath consecrated for us, through the veil, that is to say, his flesh; And having an high priest over the house of God; Let us draw near with a true heart in full assurance of faith . . ." (Heb. 10:19–22).

CHAPTERS 18 AND 19

THEME: Sign at potter's house

Now we go with Jeremiah down to the potter's house. For folk who are sophisticated and hardened in sin it is difficult to get them to listen to the Word of God; so God has a sign for the nation of Judah, and He has an object lesson for you and me.

> **The word which came to Jeremiah from the LORD, saying,**
>
> **Arise, and go down to the potter's house, and there I will cause thee to hear my words.**
>
> **Then I went down to the potter's house, and, behold, he wrought a work on the wheels.**
>
> **And the vessel that he made of clay was marred in the hand of the potter: so he made it again another vessel, as seemed good to the potter to make it.**
>
> **Then the word of the LORD came to me, saying,**
>
> **O house of Israel, cannot I do with you as this potter? saith the LORD. Behold, as the clay is in the potter's hand, so are ye in mine hand, O house of Israel [Jer. 18:1–6].**

One Sunday evening a potter, who also was one of our radio listeners, came to put on a demonstration for the congregation at an evening service. He brought in a potter's wheel which was operated by a foot pedal, and on that wheel he put clay. While I was giving the message, he molded the clay into a vessel. It was a very simple experiment, but I never repeated it—the congregation that evening was so intent on watching the potter that I don't think anyone heard my message!

Many years before this, when I was a seminary student, traveling from my home in Tennessee to the seminary at Dallas, Texas, I had to cross the state of Arkansas, and always passed by a large pottery plant near Arkadelphia. One day we took time out (several other fellows were traveling with me) to stop and see the pottery being made.

There were two very impressive and striking sights there that I have not forgotten. Behind this plant was as ugly a patch of mud as I've ever seen. It was shapeless and gooey. It looked hopeless to me. Out in front of the plant they had a display room, and in that room were some of the most exquisite vessels I have ever seen.

Then we went inside the plant, and there we saw many potters at work. There they stood, bent over many wheels which were power-driven. They didn't even have to use foot pedals; so they could give their full attention to working with that helpless, hopeless, ugly, mushy, messy clay. They were intent on transforming it and translating it into objects of art. The difference between that mass of mud out back and those lovely vessels in the display room were these men, the potters, working over their wheels.

Now it was to such a place that God sent this man Jeremiah. He sent him down to see a sermon. Actually it is a very simple sermon. It is easy to make identification in this very wonderful living parable that Jeremiah gives us. We have no difficulty in identifying the potter, and we have no difficulty in identifying the clay. In fact, God does it for us. God is the Potter, and Israel is the clay in particular here. Also it is very easy to make application to mankind in general and to each individual personally. Each individual is the clay. If I may be personal, you are clay on the Potter's wheel. Regardless of what else may be said about you, you are clay today on the Potter's wheel—as is every man who has ever lived on this earth.

The figure of the potter and clay is carried over in the New Testament. We find Paul in his epistle to the Romans using the same simile: "Hath not the potter power over the clay, of the same lump to make one vessel unto honour, and another unto dishonour?" (Rom. 9:21). Then Paul used the other side of this very wonderful figure of speech when he wrote to Timothy: "If a man therefore purge himself from these, he shall be a vessel unto honour, sanctified, and meet for the master's use, and prepared unto every good work" (2 Tim. 2:21). So we see that this figure is carried all the way through the Word of God.

Now notice what the potter did. He was fashioning a vessel, and it became marred in his hands. It wouldn't yield. The clay has to be just the right texture. Maybe it was too hard or too soft. So he pitched it aside. Then later he picked it up and made it into another kind of vessel.

There are two things we want to see in this section: the power of the potter and the personality of the clay.

POWER OF THE POTTER

Like a giant Potter, God took clay and formed man, the physical part of man. "And the LORD God formed man of the dust of the ground, and breathed into his nostrils the breath of life; and man became a living soul" (Gen. 2:7). God was the Potter.

Now let's go down to the potter's house and stand with Jeremiah as we watch the potter at work. The potter has a wheel, an old-fashioned one. He works the pedal with his foot to make the wheel turn. As he pedals, his hands are deftly, artistically working with the clay, and attempting to form out of it a work of art.

Note, now, the first principle: God is sovereign.

The potter is absolute. That is, he has power over the clay and that power is unlimited. No clay can stop the potter, nor can it question his right. No clay can resist his will, nor "say him nay," nor alter his plans. The clay cannot speak back to him. You remember the delightful little story we heard in the nursery about the gingerbread boy that talked back. But the clay can't talk back.

I recall a very whimsical story of a little boy who was playing in the mud down by a brook. He was attempting to make a man. He worked on him and had gotten pretty well along when his mother called him. They were going downtown and he must come along. He wanted to stay, but she insisted that he come. By this time he had finished his mud man except for one arm. But he had to leave. While he was in town with his mother and father, he saw a one-armed man. He eyed him for awhile. Finally he went up to him and said, "Why did you leave before I finished you?"

The clay on the potter's wheel can't get up when it wants to. The clay on the potter's wheel can't talk back. The clay on the potter's wheel is not able to do anything. It can only yield to the potter's hand.

Nowhere, I repeat, *nowhere* will you find such a graphic picture of the sovereignty of God than in this. Man, the clay upon the potter's wheel, and God, the Potter. You won't find anything quite like this.

And our contemporary generation resists it because this is the day of the rights of man. We are hearing a great deal today about freedom, and every group is insisting upon its freedom—freedom to protest, freedom to do what it chooses. We seem to have forgotten about the rights of God. Today men will permit a racketeering gangster to plead the fifth amendment because we must protect his rights. God has incontestable authority. His will is inexorable, it is inflexible, and it will prevail. He has irresistible ability to form and fashion this universe to suit Himself. He can form this little earth on which we live to suit Himself. And, my friend, you, an individual, and I, an individual, can be nothing but clay in His hands. He has power to carry through His will and He answers to no one. He has no board of directors. He has no voters to whom He must respond. He has absolute authority. He is *God*. You and I live in a universe that is running to please God. And the rebellion of little man down here on this speck of dust that we live on is a "tempest in a teapot"! Our little earth, as we see in the pictures taken from the moon, is just a speck in the infinity of space. And, my friend, God rides triumphantly in His own chariot.

You will find that the Word of God has some very definite things to say concerning Him: "Thou wilt say then unto me, Why doth he yet find fault? For who hath resisted his will? Nay but, O man, who art thou that repliest against God? Shall the thing formed say to him that formed it, Why hast thou made me thus? Hath not the potter power over the clay, of the same lump to make one vessel unto honour, and another unto dishonour?" (Rom. 9:19–21).

It was Bengel who wrote this: "The Jews thought that in no case could they be abandoned by God, and in no case could the Gentiles be received by God." And Dr. Lange, the great German expositor, said: "When man goes the length of making to himself a god whom he affects to bind by his own rights, God then puts on His majesty, and appears in all His reality as a free God, before whom man is a mere nothing, like the clay in the hand of the potter. Such was Paul's attitude when acting as God's advocate, in his suit with Jewish Pharisaism."

God is absolute!

PERSONALITY OF THE CLAY

Now for a moment let's look at the personality of the clay. I realize someone will be saying, "Believe me, you have a mixed metaphor here! You mean to tell me that *clay* has personality?" Clay is formless, it's shapeless, it's lifeless, it's inept, it's inert, it's incapable, it's a muddy mess. The psalmist wrote, ". . . he remembereth that we are dust" (Ps. 103:14). Dr. George Gill used to say in class, "God remembers that we are dust, but man sometimes forgets it, and he gets stuck on himself. And when dust gets stuck on itself, it's mud." We do sometimes forget this, but God remembers we are dust. I look at the clay on that wheel down at the potter's house. That clay has no wish; it has no rights; it has no inherent ability. It is helpless, and it is hopeless.

The Scriptures confirm this. Listen to Paul in Ephesians 2:1. Although he is writing to the Ephesians, it can apply to you and me as well: ". . . you . . . who were *dead* in trespasses and sins" (italics mine). That's man. Then he amplifies this later on in the same chapter: ". . . having no hope, and without God in the world" (Eph. 2:12). That clay on the potter's wheel is no different. Then Paul said to the Romans, "For when we were yet without strength, in due time Christ died for the ungodly" (Rom. 5:6).

You and I need to recognize that our God is a sovereign God and that we are the clay. We were dead in trespasses and sin, without strength. God is the Potter with the power. "So then it is not of him that willeth, nor of him that runneth, but of God that sheweth mercy" (Rom. 9:16). God is the One who is in charge. None of us has any claim on God. "For he saith to Moses, I will have mercy on whom I will have mercy, and I will have compassion on whom I will have compassion" (Rom. 9:15).

When Moses pleaded with God, God said to him, "Moses, I'm going to hear you, but I'm not going to hear you because you are Moses; I am going to hear you because I extend mercy." That is the reason God heard him. God is not obligated to save any man. God is free to act as He wishes. He is righteous, and He is holy. This is a lost world, and it could remain like that, and no one would have the right to raise a question.

Now look at the other side of the coin. Let's talk now about the power of the clay and the personality of the potter. This is the other side. "And the vessel that he made of clay was marred in the hand of the potter: so he made it again another vessel, as seemed good to the potter to make it." There is not only a principle here which is that God is sovereign, but also there is a purpose here.

POWER OF THE CLAY

Look now at the power of the clay. That clay on the potter's wheel is like Browning's "dance of plastic circumstance." This wheel is the wheel of circumstance. That's what it is!

I do not believe that life's big decisions are made in a church sanctuary. I believe they are made out in the work-a-day world—in the office, in the school, in the workshop, at the crossroads of life—there is where the Potter is working with the clay. There is the place He is working with you, my friend.

You and I live in a world that seems to have no purpose or meaning at all. Multitudes of people see no purpose in life whatever and find confusion on every hand. Someone has expressed it in a little jingle:

> In a day of illusions
> And utter confusions,
> Upon our delusions
> We base our conclusions.
>   —Author unknown

How true that is of life today!

Look away, for a moment, from the potter's wheel. Behind him we see shelf upon shelf of works of art. Those objects of beauty were one time on the potter's wheel as clay—clay that yielded to the potter's hand. Once they all were a shapeless mass of mud. What happened? That lifeless clay was under the hand of the potter, and as the wheel of circumstance turned, he molded and made them into the vessels that now stand on display.

I outlined the Book of Jeremiah for our Thru the Bible Radio program while my wife and I were down at Fort Myers in Florida. We had an apartment there for a few days. Every morning we would eat breakfast in the apartment, and I would work for a few hours on Jeremiah; then we would go over to one of the islands to hunt for shells. I discovered something. There are literally thousands of varieties of shells. I didn't dream there were so many. Anything God does He does in profusion. My wife bought a book on shells, and we identified many of them.

In my hand I am holding a little shell that I picked up on Sanibel Island. It is a beautiful little shell. I had been working on the eighteenth chapter of Jeremiah that morning, and when I found this, it occurred to me that the Lord was trying to say something to us. God started with just some little animal, a tiny mollusk, and around it He formed this shell. I thought, *Well, since the great Architect has spent all that time with a little shell in the bottom of the ocean, what about man today?*

Look again at those works of art which the potter has lining the shelves behind him. Don't speak disparagingly of the clay! I'm sorry for what I said about it. It has marvelous capacity and resilience. This, my friend, and I am saying it reverently, this is what the Potter wants—*clay*. He doesn't want steel. He doesn't want oil. He doesn't want rock. He wants clay. He wants something that He can put in His hand to mold and fashion. This is the stuff He is after—clay. God wants to work with human beings.

Someone may say, "Yes, but here is where the analogy breaks down. The distance between God and man is greater than between the potter and the clay." I disagree with that. Actually God is nearer man than the potter is to the clay.

This is what I mean: the clay on the wheel down at the potter's house to which Jeremiah takes us has no will. I *do!* That clay cannot cooperate with the potter. I *can!* I quoted the Genesis account of the creation of man for a purpose—God created man in His own likeness. He took man physically out of the dust of the ground; He made man. Then He breathed into his breathing-places the spirit of life, and man became a living soul. Man today has a free will, and he can exercise it. That clay has no will. But you and I do have a will; we can cooperate with the Potter.

Now I want to ask the Potter a question. What's Your purpose in putting me on the potter's wheel? Why do You bear down on me? Why do You keep working with me? Why, Potter, do You do this? I'm not being irreverent, but I am like the little gingerbread boy, I talk back. Why, O Potter, do you do this? What are You after?

Well, I go back to the potter's house. Follow me now very carefully. I do not discover the purpose, but I learn something more important than the purpose for my life. I learn that the *potter* has a purpose, which is more important to know. I watch the potter there. He is serious. He means business. He's not playing with the clay. This is his work. He is giving his time, his talents, his ability to working with the clay.

Notice again in verses 3–4: "Then I went down to the potter's house, and behold, he wrought a work on the wheels. And the vessel that he made of clay was marred in the hand of the potter: so he made it again another vessel, as seemed good to the potter to make it." My friend, this is not a cat-and-mouse operation. This is not the potter's avocation. It is his vocation. This is not his hobby. This is not something with which he is amusing himself. He knows what he is doing. This tells me that God is not playing with me today. He is not experimenting with us. He has purpose. And, friend, that comforts me. This is the second great principle we see here: the Potter has a purpose.

As a sightseer, I stand with Jeremiah, and I say, "What's he going to make?" Jeremiah says, "I don't know. Let's watch him." The sightseer cannot tell as he watches, but the potter knows. He has a plan. He knows what he is doing. The clay does not know his purpose.

But, friend, someday we will know. When He puts us on the plastic wheel of circumstance, He means to accomplish something. He has a purpose. The psalmist says, ". . . I shall be satisfied, when I awake, with thy likeness" (Ps. 17:15). Someday *I'll* be like Him! ". . . it doth not yet appear what we shall be: but we know that, when he shall appear, we shall be like him; for we shall see him as he is" (1 John 3:2). That's going to be a fair morning. That's going to be a new day. And God will be vindicated—He was not being cruel when He caused us to suffer. Some day, some glorious someday, we'll see that the Potter had a purpose in your life and in mine. Notice how Paul writes to the Ephesians. He began the second chapter with the doleful words which I have already quoted: "And you hath he quickened [made alive], who were dead in trespasses and sins" (Eph. 2:1). And if that is all, then I'm through too. But, my friend, there is more: "That in the ages to come he might shew the exceeding riches of his grace in his kindness toward us through Christ Jesus" (Eph. 2:7). In the ages to come we'll be a demonstration, and we'll be yonder on display. We will reveal what the Potter can do with lifeless clay. He gets the glory. It will be wonderful to be a vessel in the Master's hand.

PERSONALITY OF THE POTTER

In conclusion let us consider the personality of the potter. This is the most important and wonderful thing of all. To do this we must take one final look in the potter's house.

I say to Jeremiah, "The potter is a kindly looking man." Jeremiah answers, "He is. He doesn't want to hurt the clay. He wants the clay to yield because he wants to make something out of it." I gaze into the face of the potter. Oh, how intent he is. How interested he is in the clay.

Oh, what a Potter God is! If I could only see my Potter! But Scripture says I cannot see God. Philip asked the question, which I certainly would have asked, when he said to Jesus, ". . . Lord, shew us the Father, and it sufficeth us" (John 14:8). The Lord Jesus said to him, ". . . he that hath seen me hath seen the Father . . ." (John 14:9).

My friend, let us look at the Potter very carefully now. See the Potter's feet as He is working them on the pedals, turning, turning that wheel of circumstance. See the hands of the Potter as He deftly, artistically, oh, so intently and delicately, kindly and lovingly works with the clay. I look at Him. Those feet have spike wounds in them. And there are nail prints in those hands.

That's not all.

I turn over to Matthew's Gospel and read: "Then Judas, which had betrayed him, when he saw that he was condemned, repented himself, and brought again the thirty pieces of silver to the chief priests and elders, Saying, I have sinned in that I have betrayed the innocent blood. And they said, What is that to us? see thou to that. And he cast down the pieces of silver in the temple, and departed, and went and hanged himself. And the chief priests took the silver pieces, and said, It is not lawful for to put them into the treasury, because it is the price of blood. And they took counsel, and bought with them the potter's field, to bury strangers in. Wherefore that field was called, The field of blood, unto this day. Then was fulfilled that which was spoken by Jeremy the prophet, saying, And they took the thirty pieces of silver, the price of him that was valued, whom they of the children of Israel did value; And gave them for the potter's field, as the Lord appointed me" (Matt. 27:3–10).

Two verses startle me: "And they took counsel, and bought with them the potter's field, to bury strangers in. Wherefore that field was called, The field of blood, unto this day." They probably did not know what they were doing when they called it the field of blood, but I hope you don't miss it. This Potter is more wonderful than any other potter. He shed His blood that He might go into that field and take those broken pieces and put them again on His potter's wheel to make them again another vessel.

Just this past week I talked with a woman who has a broken home and a broken life. Is God through with her? Is He through with us when we make a failure of our lives? Oh, no. He's not through with us—that is, if the clay will yield to Him. All that is necessary is the clay yielding to the Potter. He paid the price for the field, it's a field of blood. You may look back on your life and say, "Oh, what failure! I don't think God could use me." My friend, He is working with those broken pieces today, and He'll work with you if you'll let Him. He has already paid the price for your redemption. You can't make anything out of yourself for Him, and I can't either, but He can take us and put us on the wheel of circumstance and shape us into a vessel of honor.

We are the clay; He is the Potter.

THE SIGN OF THE BROKEN VESSEL

In the first verse of chapter 19 God sends Jeremiah to get a potter's earthen bottle and tells him to take elders of the people and of the priests with him as witnesses.

> **And go forth unto the valley of the son of Hinnom, which is by the entry of the east gate, and proclaim there the words that I shall tell thee [Jer. 19:2].**

"The valley of the son of Hinnom" was at this time the place where the horrible worship of Moloch was conducted. God spells it out for them—

> **Because they have forsaken me, and have estranged this place, and have burned incense in it unto other gods, whom neither they nor their fathers have known, nor the kings of Judah, and have filled this place with the blood of innocents;**
>
> **They have built also the high places of Baal, to burn their sons with fire for burnt offerings unto Baal, which I commanded not, nor spake it, neither came it into my mind [Jer. 19:4–5].**

Because of these things, God says that the valley of the son of Hinnom would soon be known as the valley of slaughter, because as they had killed their children as offerings to Baal and Moloch, God would allow their enemies to kill them there (see vv. 6–9).

After pronouncing this frightful judgment upon the people of Jerusalem, God directed Jeremiah to break the clay bottle in the sight of the witnesses—

> **And shalt say unto them, Thus saith the LORD of hosts; Even so will I break this people and this city, as one breaketh a potter's vessel, that cannot be made whole again: and they shall bury them in Tophet, till there be no place to bury [Jer. 19:11].**

Returning from Tophet, or the valley of Hinnom, Jeremiah went to the court of the Lord's house and gave this final word:

> **Thus saith the LORD of hosts, the God of Israel; Behold, I will bring upon this city and upon all her towns all the evil that I have pronounced against it, because they have hardened their necks, that they might not hear my words [Jer. 19:15].**

He had warned, pleaded, and entreated, but their hearts were unrelenting. The clay had resisted the hand of the Potter too long. Very soon the enemy would come and shatter the nation in pieces.

CHAPTERS 20—22

THEME: *Jeremiah's persecution and prophecies during Zedekiah's reign*

When Jeremiah went down to Tophet and broke the bottle as the Lord had told him to do, the message he gave to the people of Judah was that they were going into captivity. Josiah, the great and good king, is dead, and he has been followed by Jehoahaz and Jehoiakim. Zedekiah, the last king of Judah, is now on the throne. He is the worst and the weakest of all the kings who ever ruled Judah. It is during his reign that the Babylonian captivity prophesied by Jeremiah will take place.

We will now see a change take place in the life and ministry of Jeremiah. When he gives out the Word of God, he's adamant, he's strong, and he's hard-nosed, but personally, as a man, he has a very tender heart. When his beloved friend Josiah died, Chronicles records that Jeremiah wept for him. The three evil kings who followed Josiah reject the ministry of Jeremiah in a very definite way. He is given a cold shoulder, and his message is absolutely ignored, but he has not been persecuted personally. As we come to chapter 20, we will find Jeremiah being personally and physically persecuted for the first time.

> **Now Pashur the son of Immer the priest, who was also chief governor in the house of the LORD, heard that Jeremiah prophesied these things.**
>
> **Then Pashur smote Jeremiah the prophet, and put him in the stocks that were in the high gate of Benjamin, which was by the house of the LORD [Jer. 20:1–2].**

Notice with whom the persecution originates: it began in organized religion. Today the Word of God is being hurt and hindered the most by the organized, liberal church which has rejected the Word of God.

They will align themselves with some very shady characters boasting of their brotherhood, their love for everyone, and their broad-mindedness. But when it comes to accepting a fundamentalist, someone who stands for the Word of God, I have found that their broad-mindedness and love disappears. There is more opposition to the furtherance of the gospel originating in the organized church than there is in the liquor industry or in any political group that I know of today. This physical persecution of Jeremiah began in the organized religion of his day.

> **And it came to pass on the morrow, that Pashur brought forth Jeremiah out of the stocks. Then said Jeremiah unto him, The LORD hath not called thy name Pashur, but Magor-missabib [Jer. 20:3].**

"Magor-missabib"—that's quite a name, and it means "terror on every side." Jeremiah is telling Pashur that there is terror in store for him and for everyone connected with him.

> **For thus saith the LORD, Behold, I will make thee a terror to thyself, and to all thy friends: and they shall fall by the sword of their enemies, and thine eyes shall behold it: and I will give all Judah into the hand of the king of Babylon, and he shall carry them captive into Babylon, and shall slay them with the sword [Jer. 20:4].**

This is now the prophecy that Jeremiah will emphasize again and again: the southern kingdom is going into captivity, and nothing can stop it. God has said that it would not help if even Moses or Samuel were alive. It is too late. The people have gone too far in their rejection of God as has been revealed by the actions of the present king and the two who have been on the throne ahead of him.

We need to consider what has happened to Jeremiah. He has been ignored and rejected, but up to this point he has not been persecuted physically. But now he is, and because of all this—remember that his message is breaking his own heart—he decides he will turn in his resignation to God. Your heart cannot help but go out to this man. He is not indifferent to what is happening. He feels all this very deeply, and it is sapping his strength. I think he may even have been on the verge of a nervous breakdown.

Then I said, I will not make mention of him, nor speak any more in his name. But his word was in mine heart as a burning fire shut up in my bones, and I was weary with forbearing, and I could not stay [Jer. 20:9].

What Jeremiah is saying is this: "The message is breaking my heart, and all it has earned for me is the persecution of the religious rulers and the rejection of the people; therefore I'm resigning." But when he attempted to resign he found that the Word of God was in his bones like a fire. He says, "I had to speak out. I couldn't forbear."

Such urgency to speak should be the mark of any man who is giving out the Word of God. How do *you* really feel about it? Is your ministry just a job you have, or is your heart really in it? If you love the Word of God and you really want to give it out, then you would feel pretty bad if you didn't have that privilege and opportunity. Unless it really means something to you, I don't believe you should be attempting to give out the Word of God.

You can understand the conflict that is going on in the heart of Jeremiah, and he indulges in something that seems to have been a habit with God's men in the Old Testament. He does something that Jonah did, that Job did, and Elijah did. He begins to sing an old song that won't do him any good. It's the blues, the religious blues: "Why was I born?" A lot of folk sing that song. Listen to Jeremiah:

Cursed be the day wherein I was born: let not the day wherein my mother bare me be blessed.

Cursed be the man who brought tidings to my father, saying, A man child is born unto thee; making him very glad [Jer. 20:14–15].

Oh boy, does Jeremiah hate himself and wish he had never been born!

> **Wherefore came I forth out of the womb to see labour and sorrow, that my days should be consumed with shame? [Jer. 20:18].**

Behold, it's the old story: Why was I born? Elijah crawled up under a juniper tree and said, "Let me die!" (see 1 Kings 19:4). Job wanted to die and cursed the day he was born. Old Jonah got pretty downhearted about everything, and he also wanted to die. Well, to wish that you had not been born is about as foolish as anything you could wish. My friend, you have already been born, and there is nothing you can do about it. You can sing the blues that you want to die, but you will never die by wishing it—no one ever has. Jeremiah is way down, is he not? You wish that you could put your arm around him, pat him on the back, and encourage him somehow. He is so discouraged; yet he wants to give out the Word of God.

Chapters 21 through 29 contain the prophecies delivered during the reign of Zedekiah, the last king of Judah. This will bring us right down to the time of the destruction of Jerusalem and the captivity. There is not a harsher message than the one Jeremiah gives here in chapters 21 and 22.

ANSWER TO ZEDEKIAH REGARDING NEBUCHADNEZZAR

> **The word which came unto Jeremiah from the Lord, when king Zedekiah sent unto him Pashur the son of Melchiah, and Zephaniah the son of Maaseiah the priest, saying,**

> **Inquire, I pray thee, of the Lord for us; for Nebuchadrezzar king of Babylon maketh war against us; if so be that the Lord will deal with us according to all his wondrous works, that he may go up from us [Jer. 21:1–2].**

It is interesting that when Zedekiah got into real trouble he went to the man he knew was giving the Word of God. He went right past

Pashur and his crowd—he didn't seek help from organized religion. I find that a great many people today belong to a liberal church, but they listen to a Bible broadcast on the radio. For some strange reason they feel they can reconcile those two things. My friend, when you are in trouble nothing is going to satisfy you but the Word of God.

Zedekiah comes to Jeremiah but he doesn't get any comfort from him at all. Jeremiah tells him that Nebuchadnezzar is coming and he will destroy the city unless there is a turning to God. Jeremiah really lays it on the line to him.

> **And unto this people thou shalt say, Thus saith the Lord; Behold, I set before you the way of life, and the way of death [Jer. 21:8].**

That is exactly what God says to you today about His salvation provided in the Lord Jesus Christ. God says that He gave His Son to die for you, to pay the penalty of your sin. He arose so that you might have righteousness. If you are to be saved, you must be in Him. You get into Him by the baptism of the Holy Spirit when you put your trust in Jesus Christ as your Savior. When you do that, you become a child of God. God says, "This is My way that I offer to you. You can take it or leave it. I set before you life and death." That is the way God has put it. God also pleads with tears in His eyes.

Now the choice before the people of Judah was to stay in the city and die or to surrender to the king of Babylon and live.

> **He that abideth in this city shall die by the sword, and by the famine, and by the pestilence: but he that goeth out, and falleth to the Chaldeans that besiege you, he shall live, and his life shall be unto him for a prey.**
>
> **For I have set my face against this city for evil, and not for good, saith the Lord: it shall be given into the hand of the king of Babylon, and he shall burn it with fire [Jer. 21:9–10].**

King Zedekiah didn't follow through. He was a weakling and the worst of the kings. He does not turn to God at all. He evidently thought something like this: *Well, look, God didn't let Nebuchadnezzar destroy this city when Jehoiachin was on the throne and he was about as bad as I am. Why should it happen now?*

JUDGMENT OF JEHOIAKIM

Chapter 22, therefore, contains what I feel is the harshest judgment that is pronounced in the Word of God. It is harsher than the judgment pronounced by God upon Cain or by the Lord Jesus upon Judas. It is frightful, and at the same time one of the most remarkable prophecies in the Word of God.

Before we consider the judgment against Coniah, or Jehoiachin, there is first the judgment against his father, Jehoiakim. He was an evil ruler also, but during his reign there was prosperity. The rich were getting richer, and the poor were being ground underfoot. It is very interesting that the Word of God has so much to say about the poor. God pays so much attention to them, both in the Old and New Testaments, that we cannot ignore it.

This begins God's message concerning Jehoiakim:

Woe unto him that buildeth his house by unrighteousness, and his chambers by wrong; that useth his neighbour's service without wages, and giveth him not for his work [Jer. 22:13].

Men were getting rich through wrong methods. The poor were being underpaid.

That saith, I will build me a wide house and large chambers, and cutteth him out windows; and it is cieled with cedar, and painted with vermilion.

Shalt thou reign, because thou closest thyself in cedar? did not thy father eat and drink, and do judgment and justice, and then it was well with him? [Jer. 22:14–15].

"Thy father"—Jeremiah is referring back to Josiah, the good king, and this is what he says about him:

> **He judged the cause of the poor and needy; then it was well with him: was not this to know me? saith the Lord.**

> **But thine eyes and thine heart are not but for thy covetousness, and for to shed innocent blood, and for oppression, and for violence, to do it [Jer. 22:16–17].**

Josiah had "judged the cause of the poor and needy"; but in Jehoiakim's day the rich were getting richer by wrong methods, and the poor were getting poorer.

God has a great deal to say on this subject. Jeremiah called attention to the fact that the rich men were heaping up wealth by the labor of others and treading down the poor. In their pride and in their arrogance they built themselves palaces and lived as though God had forgotten their iniquitous means for the acquisition of their wealth. In the New Testament we read: "Go to now, ye rich men, weep and howl for your miseries that shall come upon you. Your riches are corrupted, and your garments are motheaten. Your gold and silver is cankered; and the rust of them shall be a witness against you . . ." (James 5:1–3). There are two things for which God condemns the rich: the way they get their money, and the way they spend their money or the way they use it.

Have you noticed that everything is slanted for the rich man? I find that I am paying more taxes than some men who are worth a million dollars. You would think I am a millionaire judging from the taxes I must pay! The tax laws are geared to protect the rich. The politicians gear everything in favor of the rich, those who have given to their political campaigns. That is what the rich people support. Most of them don't give to the work of the Lord; they don't give in order to get out the Word of God. God notices that. He notices when the rich get rich at the expense of the poor, and He notices when they spend their wealth on themselves, building palaces to live in.

Very frankly, it is sinful to live in a mansion when there are so many people in such poverty. I do not believe a Christian should do that. There are a lot of poor Christians who need help from the wealthier Christians. And I am not sure that Christian organizations should have plush and luxurious accommodations either.

May I say also that there is too much of a tendency for religion to cater to the rich. I often hear preachers boast that they have a millionaire or two in their congregation. I'd like to know what they are doing to get the Word of God out.

I played golf with a man who is reported to be worth twenty million dollars. I was told he might be interested in supporting our radio broadcast. After he asked me about it, I told him all about the broadcast and the needs of the program. He was interested, and he assured me he listens to the broadcast. Do you know how much support he has given the program? Not one dime. I give this isolated case as an example, but I would hate to be a Christian who left a million dollars when I died and have to face the Lord to account for what I had done with my money. I do not think this means we are not to enjoy what the Lord gives us—the comforts that He has made possible—but if He has given you wealth, He is going to hold you responsible for using it for His glory.

"He judged the cause of the poor and needy . . . was not this to know me? saith the Lord." God says, "Josiah knew Me, and he knew that he could not be My follower and not have a concern for the poor and needy." God says that He has a concern for these people.

Do you know who are the two groups of people that are the hardest to reach with the gospel? They are the very rich and the very poor. God wants to equalize that because He wants them to hear the gospel and be saved. He wants the rich way up at the top to help those way down at the bottom. And He is concerned that both be reached with the Word of God.

The fundamental social problem in America today is not a racial or a class struggle. It is a question of the rich and the poor. Communism would never have risen in the world if it were not for the struggle between the filthy rich and the very poor. And it is this inequality that God says He judges.

JUDGMENT OF CONIAH

Now we come to the very frightful and harsh judgment against the man Coniah.

> **As I live, saith the LORD, though Coniah the son of Jehoiakim king of Judah were the signet upon my right hand, yet would I pluck thee thence;**
>
> **And I will give thee into the hand of them that seek thy life, and into the hand of them whose face thou fearest, even into the hand of Nebuchadrezzar king of Babylon, and into the hand of the Chaldeans [Jer. 22:24–25].**

"Coniah" is Jehoiachin who was also called Jeconian. Why does God call him Coniah? It is because the "Je" in Jeconiah stands for Jehovah. God is saying, "Don't identify Me with that man!" He goes on to say, "Why, if he were the ring on My finger, I would throw him away!"

> **Is this man Coniah a despised broken idol? is he a vessel wherein is no pleasure? wherefore are they cast out, he and his seed, and are cast into a land which they know not?**
>
> **O earth, earth, earth, hear the word of the LORD.**
>
> **Thus saith the LORD, Write ye this man childless, a man that shall not prosper in his days: for no man of his seed shall prosper, sitting upon the throne of David, and ruling any more in Judah [Jer. 22:28–30].**

God cries to the whole earth to be His witness: No descendant of Coniah will sit on the throne of David or rule anymore in Judah. This is one reason that Joseph could not have been the father of Jesus. Joseph was in the line of Jeconiah, and God says no child of that line will sit on the throne of David.

Does that mean the throne of David would be vacant from then on? Listen to another prophecy: "For thus saith the LORD; David shall never want a man to sit upon the throne of the house of Israel" (Jer. 33:17). There *will* be Someone on the throne of David, but He will not be a descendant in the line of Jeconiah. In Jeremiah 36:30 we read: "Therefore thus saith the LORD of Jehoiakim king of Judah; He shall have none to sit upon the throne of David: and his dead body shall be cast out in the day to the heat, and in the night to the frost." I remind you that Jehoiakim was the father of Jeconiah. God cut off that line.

Now the remarkable thing is that there are two recorded genealogies of Jesus Christ, and there is a reason for that. The one recorded in Matthew chapter 1 leads to Joseph. It comes from David, through Solomon and *Jeconiah,* to Joseph. Joseph's line gave to Jesus the *legal* title to the throne. But Joseph was not the father of Jesus. Jesus is not a descendant of that line. The second genealogy is in Luke 3:23–38. This is the genealogy of Mary, and it does not come through Solomon but comes through another son of David, Nathan. There is no curse and no judgment on that line. The Lord Jesus Christ was virgin born, and He came through Mary's line. That is where He got the *blood* title to the throne of David. I find this to be one of the most remarkable things that has occurred in this world!

That is why God calls the earth to listen: "O earth, earth, earth, hear the word of the LORD." He wants the earth to see that this is the way He has worked it out. God's purposes will not be thwarted. He is able to bring judgment upon whomever He wills; yet He was able to fulfill His promise that the coming Messiah would be a descendant of King David.

CHAPTERS 23 AND 24

THEME: Bright light in a dark day and parable of two baskets of figs

Every cloud has a silver lining, so the song says, and the dark clouds of the previous chapter also have a silver lining. It never got so dark that the prophets could not see light at the end of the tunnel. After chapter 22, which has the harshest judgment in the Bible against Coniah, the sun breaks through. However, we'll have two more verses before we see the sun—

> **Woe be unto the pastors that destroy and scatter the sheep of my pasture! saith the LORD [Jer. 23:1].**

The "pastors" here are not preachers. He will speak about the religious rulers later on. Here the pastors refer to the kings, the politicians, the people who are ruling, the ones who are responsible for the laws of the land. God says, "Woe be unto them."

> **Therefore thus saith the LORD God of Israel against the pastors that feed my people; Ye have scattered my flock, and driven them away, and have not visited them: behold, I will visit upon you the evil of your doings, saith the LORD [Jer. 23:2].**

God said He was going to judge them, and He did.
Now the sun breaks through:

> **And I will gather the remnant of my flock out of all countries whither I have driven them, and will bring them again to their folds; and they shall be fruitful and increase.**

> And I will set up shepherds over them which shall feed them: and they shall fear no more, nor be dismayed, neither shall they be lacking, saith the LORD [Jer. 23:3–4].

God says, "The day is coming when I intend to take over, and when I do, the poor will be taken care of." This refers specifically to the return of the Jews to their land after the present dispensation has closed and the church has been raptured. At that time the King whom they once rejected will tenderly set over them faithful shepherds. It will be an altogether different type of government from what we have in the world now.

> Behold, the days come, saith the LORD, that I will raise unto David a righteous Branch, and a King shall reign and prosper, and shall execute judgment and justice in the earth [Jer. 23:5].

There is a King coming in David's line. The king, Coniah and all of his line, although they are in David's line, shall be rejected and cut off. However, no one can destroy God's purpose, although they may think they can. God knows what He will do. We know from the New Testament that through another line, the line of Nathan, another son of David, came a peasant by the name of Mary, a girl up in Nazareth, who bore Jesus, the Messiah, the King. When Jesus presented Himself to the world, He said, ". . . Repent: for the kingdom of heaven is at hand" (Matt. 4:17). Since you can't have a kingdom without the king, in effect He was saying to the people, "Your King is here!" The people rejected the King, but He had the last word. He said that someday the King would come back and set up that kingdom.

> In his days Judah shall be saved, and Israel shall dwell safely: and this is his name whereby he shall be called, THE LORD OUR RIGHTEOUSNESS [Jer. 23:6].

Have you ever heard of this as a plank in a political platform? I have never heard a candidate claim that he is righteous and that he will follow God's plan and program for government. I've heard politicians make almost every other claim under the sun but that one! They wouldn't dare make it. But *righteousness* will characterize the Kingdom when the Lord Jesus Christ reigns.

> **Therefore, behold, the days come, saith the LORD, that they shall no more say, The LORD liveth, which brought up the children of Israel out of the land of Egypt;**
>
> **But, the LORD liveth, which brought up and which led the seed of the house of Israel out of the north country, and from all countries whither I had driven them; and they shall dwell in their own land [Jer. 23:7–8].**

This is one of the most remarkable prophecies in the Word of God. The oldest religious holiday celebrated today is the Jewish Passover. Regardless of whether the Jew is reformed or orthodox, he remembers the Passover, because it is the celebration of the miraculous deliverance of the Jews out of Egypt. Now God is saying, "The day is coming when I will bring them back into their land that they will *forget* the deliverance out of Egypt and they will *remember* this new deliverance which I intend to accomplish." It will be that tremendous! Obviously God is not through with the nation Israel, my friend.

> **Thus saith the LORD of hosts, Hearken not unto the words of the prophets that prophesy unto you: they make you vain: they speak a vision of their own heart, and not out of the mouth of the LORD.**
>
> **They say still unto them that despise me, The LORD hath said, Ye shall have peace; and they say unto every one that walketh after the imagination of his own heart, No evil shall come upon you [Jer. 23:16–17].**

The false prophets persisted in prophesying peace. God repudiates them. Today there are dreamers who are talking about how *they* are going to bring in world peace, and all of them are talking along that same line. God says, "You won't do it—you can't do it." God said through Isaiah, "There is no peace . . . unto the wicked" (Isa. 48:22). The problem is not that the people don't want peace; the trouble is that the heart of man is desperately wicked. We don't realize how bad we really are. Wicked men in power today cannot bring peace on this earth. If they could, it would be a contradiction of the Word of God.

God turns now to the religious rulers.

> **I have not sent these prophets, yet they ran: I have not spoken to them, yet they prophesied [Jer. 23:21].**

He has already said you can't trust the political rulers. They cannot bring in peace. They ignore the poor. Now God says that He did not send the bunch of prophets that were filling the land in that day. God denies that their message comes from Him. God rejected both the political rulers and the religious rulers.

Today I believe that God would say the same thing to the world. Who is seeking God in our day? The religious rulers of the world are out for religion. They are religious up to their eyebrows and are so pious, but how many of them are seeking out the living and true God?

> **Therefore, behold, I am against the prophets, saith the LORD, that steal my words every one from his neighbour [Jer. 23:30].**

The contemporary liberal theologians are casting reflections upon the Word of God, saying it is not truly the Word of God, thereby stealing it out of the hearts of the people. I would cringe if I were one of the godless college professors or godless preachers who is wrecking the faith of believers. God says that He is going to do something about it someday. God is in no hurry—don't be deceived because God's judgment against an evil work is not executed speedily. That day of judgment is coming. It is in the hearts of the sons of man to do evil. They think they are getting by with it. God says, "I have eternity ahead of Me, and I am still running this show. The time will come when I will judge the religious rulers."

Chapter 24 is a sort of appendix, relating a vision given after Jeconiah had been carried away into captivity. Therefore it was during the early part of Zedekiah's reign. In a vision Jeremiah was shown two baskets of figs (the fig tree is a well-known symbol of Judah). One basket contained good figs and the other very bad figs. They symbolized two classes of people in Judah.

> **Thus saith the LORD, the God of Israel; Like these good figs, so will I acknowledge them that are carried away captive of Judah, whom I have sent out of this place into the land of the Chaldeans for their good.**

> **For I will set mine eyes upon them for good, and I will bring them again to this land: and I will build them, and not pull them down; and I will plant them, and not pluck them up [Jer. 24:5–6].**

Notice that God had sent them away into captivity "for their good." He promises to watch over them and eventually restore them (a remnant) to their land. That their restoration to the land does not refer to the return under Ezra and Nehemiah is clear from the final words "and not pluck them up." Obviously they have been plucked up again. The reference is to their restoration during the Millennium when "they shall return unto me with their whole heart" (v. 7).

The bad figs represented Zedekiah and those who remained in Jerusalem and finally went down to Egypt in defiance of God's Word.

> **And I will deliver them to be removed into all the kingdoms of the earth for their hurt, to be a reproach and a proverb, a taunt and a curse, in all places whither I shall drive them [Jer. 24:9].**

Secular history gives us the accurate fulfillment of this prophecy which Jeremiah faithfully delivered to his people.

CHAPTER 25

THEME: God spells out seventy-year captivity

This chapter deals with a prophecy which was given about seventeen or eighteen years before that of the previous chapter. (Keep in mind that the Book of Jeremiah is not arranged in a chronological order.) The son of Josiah, Jehoiakim, was on the throne. He was very different from his godly father, as 2 Kings 24:4 records: ". . . he filled Jerusalem with innocent blood; which the Lord would not pardon."

Jeremiah makes this pointed charge:

> **And the Lord hath sent unto you all his servants the prophets, rising early and sending them; but ye have not hearkened, nor inclined your ear to hear [Jer. 25:4].**

Because they will not hear God's Word, the land will be invaded by Babylon.

> **Behold, I will send and take all the families of the north, saith the Lord, and Nebuchadrezzar the king of Babylon, my servant, and will bring them against this land, and against the inhabitants thereof, and against all these nations round about, and will utterly destroy them, and make them an astonishment, and an hissing, and perpetual desolations [Jer. 25:9].**

"Nebuchadrezzar the king of Babylon, my servant"—God calls Nebuchadnezzar His servant! (The variant spelling Nebuchadrezzar is probably more nearly correct than the common Nebuchadnezzar.) He was God's instrument of judgment.

A great many people wonder why the land of Israel is not a land flowing with milk and honey today. There is a desperate need for water in that land. God said He would make it a perpetual desolation, and He intends to let the world know that He not only judged the people but He also judged the land. There is a judgment of God upon that land specifically just as the curse of sin is on the entire earth—the earth does not produce what it is capable of producing because of the curse of sin upon it.

> **Moreover I will take from them the voice of mirth, and the voice of gladness, the voice of the bridegroom, and the voice of the bride, the sound of the millstones, and the light of the candle [Jer. 25:10].**

God will take away from them all the fun they have been having. Neither will there be any more marrying and giving in marriage. "The sound of the millstones" will cease, which means that business and commerce will end. "The light of the candle"—they won't enjoy evenings at home anymore.

> **And this whole land shall be a desolation, and an astonishment; and these nations shall serve the king of Babylon seventy years [Jer. 25:11].**

When God is dealing with the nation of Israel, He deals with the calendar. He spells out *time* in relation to their history. When God deals with the church, He does not give any times. Therefore you and I are not able to say when the Lord Jesus is coming. We have no right to say even that He is coming soon—we have not been told the *time* of His coming.

The seventy-year period of time is very significant. When the people of Israel were about to enter the land, the Lord told them that every seventh year was to be a Sabbath in which the ground was to lie fallow (see Lev. 25). Not only did God promise blessing if His Word was obeyed, but He warned of judgment if it was not. If they walked contrary to Him, He would walk contrary to them. Notice that God foresaw their disobedience: "Then shall the land enjoy her sabbaths, as long as it lieth desolate, and ye be in your enemies' land; even then shall the land rest, and enjoy her sabbaths. As long as it lieth desolate it shall rest; because it did not rest in your sabbaths, when ye dwelt upon it" (Lev. 26:34–35). For approximately 490 years the sabbatic year was not kept—seventy Sabbaths had been neglected. God says through Jeremiah that for seventy years they will live in a strange country while their land has its rest. Then after the lost sabbatic years have been made up, Israel will be permitted to return to the land. Listen to Jeremiah:

> **And it shall come to pass, when seventy years are accomplished, that I will punish the king of Babylon, and that nation, saith the LORD, for their iniquity, and the land of the Chaldeans, and will make it perpetual desolations [Jer. 25:12].**

At the time of Jeremiah this was a prophecy. It is now history. God has done that. There is no argument here.

THE WINE CUP OF FURY

At the time this prophecy was given, Nebuchadnezzar had already deported to Babylon Jehoiachin with all his nobles, soldiers, and artificers. Those who remained under Zedekiah were all paying tribute (taxes) to Babylon. All the kings after Josiah were evil. Jeremiah had pronounced final judgment—Nebuchadnezzar would come and destroy Jerusalem and take all but a small remnant into captivity. He has told them that the captivity will definitely last for seventy years. But that does not conclude his prophecy.

He gives them now a picture using the figure of the wine cup of the wrath of God. This is a figure of speech that several of the prophets used. They spoke of the sin of man as he continues in rebellion against God.

> **For thus saith the LORD God of Israel unto me; Take the wine cup of this fury at my hand, and cause all the nations, to whom I send thee, to drink it.**

> And they shall drink, and be moved, and be mad, because of the sword that I will send among them.
>
> Then took I the cup at the Lord's hand, and made all the nations to drink, unto whom the Lord had sent me [Jer. 25:15–17].

Now he lists the nations.

> To wit, Jerusalem, and the cities of Judah, and the kings thereof, and the princes thereof, to make them a desolation, an astonishment, an hissing, and a curse; as it is this day [Jer. 25:18].

First, of course, Jerusalem and the cities of Judah, the kings and the princes are mentioned. Although this especially relates to the sin of Israel, it is not confined to God's own people. All the nations of the world are guilty. Like a wine cup gets full, there is a filling up of the wrath of God.

After Israel, he mentions Egypt:

> Pharaoh king of Egypt, and his servants, and his princes, and all his people [Jer. 25:19].

Then he mentions Uz and the land of the Philistines and Ashkelon and Azzah and Ekron and Ashdod and Edom and Moab and Ammon and Tyre and Zidon and "the kings of the isles which are beyond the sea" (v. 22). They are all to take the wine cup of the wrath of God. Man's sin and continuous rebellion against God is like a wine cup which is filling up with God's anger. When it is full, the judgment of God will break upon the earth.

> Therefore thou shalt say unto them, Thus saith the Lord of hosts, the God of Israel; Drink ye, and be drunken, and spue, and fall, and rise no more, because of the sword which I will send among you [Jer. 25:27].

He makes them drink that cup, which is, of course, the judgment of God. All of the nations in the area of Israel and beyond it were to be judged of God because they had gotten so far away from Him. This reveals the fact that all the nations of the world are responsible to God.

> **Therefore prophesy thou against them all these words, and say unto them, The LORD shall roar from on high, and utter his voice from his holy habitation; he shall mightily roar upon his habitation; he shall give a shout, as they that tread the grapes, against all the inhabitants of the earth [Jer. 25:30].**

The judgment would not be confined to Israel. Babylon, you see, will be God's instrument of judgment, and we know from history that Babylon did become the first great world power which dominated all the nations of the civilized world at that time.

> **Thus saith the LORD of hosts, Behold, evil shall go forth from nation to nation, and a great whirlwind shall be raised up from the coasts of the earth [Jer. 25:32].**

This is descriptive of the tremendous movement of Nebuchadnezzar, king of Babylon, as he moved out over the civilized world of his day and brought even Egypt and Tyre and Sidon—these great powers— under his sovereignty. The verses that conclude this chapter give a graphic description of the day of the Lord's anger with the nations and their "shepherds," or kings.

CHAPTERS 26—28

THEME: Message in temple court during reign of Jehoiakim and parable of yokes

You may recall that in chapter 7 Jeremiah was told to stand at the gate of the Lord's house and speak to the people. Here he is told to stand in the *court*.

> **Thus saith the LORD; stand in the court of the LORD'S house, and speak unto all the cities of Judah, which come to worship in the LORD'S house, all the words that I command thee to speak unto them; diminish not a word [Jer. 26:2].**

This is a message that he had already given in the time of Jehoiakim. Now it is repeated at the time of Zedekiah. Chapters 26—30 record the message which delivered the final words of God to these people before the captivity.

I am of the opinion that the people were still coming to the temple as usual. There was this outward show of worship, and there was prosperity in the land at that time; nobody seemed to be complaining. It looked as if God were being petulant to make such prophecies, but in actuality the people were far from God, and there was awful sin in the land. Jeremiah was to continue to cry out against this.

> **If so be they will hearken, and turn every man from his evil way, that I may repent me of the evil, which I purpose to do unto them because of the evil of their doings [Jer. 26:3].**

"That I may repent me of the evil." When God repents, it does not mean that He has changed His mind. He means that the people have changed. If the people will change, God will not judge; He will bless.

It looks as if God had changed His mind, but the fact is that God will always punish sin and will always pardon the sinner who will come to Him. That never changes. When a sinner, who has been under the judgment of God, turns to God and is blessed and saved, it looks as if God has changed His mind. However, in fact, it is the sinner who has changed his mind. God tells them that if they will change, then He will not destroy them; He will not judge them.

And thou shalt say unto them, Thus saith the LORD; If ye will not hearken to me, to walk in my law, which I have set before you,

To hearken to the words of my servants the prophets, whom I sent unto you, both rising up early, and sending them, but ye have not hearkened;

Then will I make this house like Shiloh, and will make this city a curse to all the nations of the earth [Jer. 26:4-6].

"Then will I make this house like Shiloh"—meaning that it would be destroyed.

"And will make this city a curse to all the nations of the earth"— Jerusalem has been a burden to this world, and it is at the present moment. At the time I am writing this commentary, Jerusalem does not even belong to the nation Israel; it is like a pawn on the chessboard of the earth controlled by Russia and America. God said that He would make it a burden to all nations, and He certainly has done that.

JEREMIAH THREATENED WITH DEATH

Now it came to pass, when Jeremiah had made an end of speaking all that the LORD had commanded him to speak unto all the people, that the priests and the prophets and all the people took him, saying, Thou shalt surely die [Jer. 26:8].

Things are getting bad. They have resisted the message of God through Jeremiah, and now they want to *kill* Jeremiah. Now this gets rather complicated because there are three groups in this section: the princes, the priests and the prophets, and the people.

> **Then spake the priests and the prophets unto the princes and to all the people, saying, This man is worthy to die; for he hath prophesied against this city, as ye have heard with your ears [Jer. 26:11].**

The priests and the prophets were of one mind; they had determined his death. They never changed their minds about that at all. However, the princes decided they had better hear Jeremiah, and the people who had been of the same mind as the priests and prophets came over on the side of the princes.

> **Then spake Jeremiah unto all the princes and to all the people, saying, The Lord sent me to prophesy against this house and against this city all the words that ye have heard.**
>
> **Therefore now amend your ways and your doings, and obey the voice of the Lord your God; and the Lord will repent him of the evil that he hath pronounced against you [Jer. 26:12–13].**

He makes it clear why God is threatening to judge them.

Let's keep in mind that it was considered blasphemy when Jeremiah prophesied that the city and the temple would be destroyed. This branded him as a heretic. The false prophets were saying that God would never let the temple fall. It was His temple, and Jerusalem was His city. God would not let that happen. Jeremiah said, "You are entirely wrong. You are disassociating religion from morality."

This is a problem with a number of people who are very fundamental in their belief. They make the Word of God almost a fetish. I don't believe there is anyone more fundamental in his doctrine than I am. People say that I lean backwards, I am so fundamental. But I do want to say that it is entirely wrong to divorce *morality* from your faith, be it ever so fundamental. One can make religion and the Word of God a sort of good-luck charm.

It reminds me of the story of a soldier who carried a New Testament in his pocket. The bullet hit the book in his shirt pocket, and that saved his life. Well, the book didn't stop the bullet because it was a New Testament—it could have been any kind of a book. How foolish to make the Word of God a sort of fetish.

Oh, my friend, we can't divorce our manner of life from the teachings of the Word of God and still expect His blessing. This is what the false prophets were doing. And in our day many folk are saying, "Because I am fundamental in my doctrine, no harm can come to me." Well, it *can* come to you. When you and I get away from God, He will judge us.

I point out again how interesting it is that the priests and the false prophets did not change their minds about putting Jeremiah to death. The princes did, and that is the thing that saved the life of Jeremiah. The princes were willing to hear him. It has been my experience that when a spiritual authority becomes corrupt and debased it is far more evil than when the politicians become corrupt and debased. When the civil authority is corrupt, that is bad; but when the religious authority becomes corrupt, that is a lot worse. Let me remind you that it was the *priests* who put the Lord Jesus to death on the Cross. It was the religious rulers who insisted that He must die; they were the ones who persuaded the people to shout, "Crucify Him!" And the *religious* leaders in Jeremiah's time were determined to kill him.

This reveals another fallacy: We hear the expression, *Vox populi, vox Dei*, that is, "the voice of the people is the voice of God." There are a lot of people in America who believe that. They consider public opinion as the authority. However, the mass of people is a fickle crowd that will follow one TV personality after another. It will elect a man to office if he has charisma even though he may be the biggest fool in the world and utterly corrupt in his life. The voice of the people is the very worst basis for authority. I thank God that He is not going to let the world vote the Lord Jesus into office! If God were to put it up to a public vote, Jesus Christ would never enter into His Kingdom. I rejoice that God will send the Lord Jesus to this earth to put down rebellion.

During those last troubled days of the kingdom of Judah, God is saying that the people are wrong, the princes are wrong, the priests are wrong, and the prophets are wrong. Jeremiah isn't even sure of himself; he is only sure that he is giving out the Word of God.

The Word of God is the only and final authority. People today are turning to the signs of the zodiac and the horoscope—we have mentioned the utter foolishness of that. But we find some Christians, often ministers and leaders, who feel that they are a final authority. I appreciate this Book of Jeremiah. It helps me, because I confess that the more I study the Word of God the more aware I am of my own ignorance of it. It disturbs me that so many men think they know it all and are the final authority.

It is said that Socrates made the statement that he was the wisest man in Athens. When asked on what grounds he made such a claim he replied that he was the wisest man because he realized that his wisdom was worthless!

The only claim I can make today is that I know I am ignorant of the Word of God. A Persian proverb puts it this way:

> He who knows not and knows not that he
>   knows not is a fool. Shun him.
> He who knows not and knows that he
>   knows not is a child. Teach him.
> He who knows and knows not that he
>   knows is asleep. Wake him.
> He who knows and knows that he knows
>   is wise. Follow him.
>   —Author unknown

I will accept the first three statements, but not the last one, because I don't think we do know. This is also Jeremiah's position—all he knows is the Word of God. Although the false prophets insist that nothing is going to happen, Jeremiah believes God, and he knows something is going to happen.

In chapter 27 the message is to go out again to all the nations that they are to yield to the king of Babylon. This time his message is illustrated—

> **Thus saith the LORD to me; Make thee bonds and yokes, and put them upon thy neck,**
>
> **And send them to the king of Edom, and to the king of Moab, and to the king of the Ammonites, and to the king of Tyrus, and to the king of Zidon, by the hand of the messengers which come to Jerusalem unto Zedekiah king of Judah [Jer. 27:2-3].**

God reminds these nations that He is the Creator and He gives power to whomever He chooses—

> **And now have I given all these lands into the hand of Nebuchadnezzar the king of Babylon, my servant; and the beasts of the field have I given him also to serve him [Jer. 27:6].**

Although God clearly told these nations to yield to the king of Babylon, they did not obey. Had they done as He said, they would have saved literally thousands of human lives—

> **And it shall come to pass, that the nation and kingdom which will not serve the same Nebuchadnezzar the king of Babylon, and that will not put their neck under the yoke of the king of Babylon, that nation will I punish, saith the LORD, with the sword, and with the famine, and with the pestilence, until I have consumed them by his hand [Jer. 27:8].**

HANANIAH, THE FALSE PROPHET

Chapter 28 continues the prophecy of the yokes. One of the false prophets, Hananiah, refutes the prophecy of Jeremiah and claims to give the true Word of the Lord:

> **Thus speaketh the Lord of hosts, the God of Israel, saying, I have broken the yoke of the king of Babylon.**
>
> **Within two full years will I bring again into this place all the vessels of the Lord's house, that Nebuchadnezzar king of Babylon took away from this place, and carried them to Babylon:**
>
> **And I will bring again to this place Jeconiah the son of Jehoiakim king of Judah, with all the captives of Judah, that went into Babylon, saith the Lord: for I will break the yoke of the king of Babylon [Jer. 28:2–4].**

Well, Jeremiah made it clear that Hananiah was not a prophet of God and that he was giving the people a lie. Hananiah actually took the wooden yoke from off Jeremiah's neck and broke it, saying, "Thus saith the Lord; Even so will I break the yoke of Nebuchadnezzar king of Babylon from the neck of all nations within the space of two full years" (v. 11).

As a judgment upon him, God said to tell him that he would die within the year. Notice what happened:

> **Then said the prophet Jeremiah unto Hananiah the prophet, Hear now, Hananiah; The Lord hath not sent thee; but thou makest this people to trust in a lie.**
>
> **Therefore thus saith the Lord; Behold, I will cast thee from off the face of the earth: this year thou shalt die, because thou hast taught rebellion against the Lord.**
>
> **So Hananiah the prophet died the same year in the seventh month [Jer. 28:15–17].**

He died, just as God said he would.

You would think this would alert the people and they would say, "Look, Jeremiah is the one who is calling the shots. Jeremiah is the one who is giving us God's Word." However, they were not convinced, but went on in their rebellion against the Word of God.

Judah listened to the wrong voices, and we have done the same thing in our own recent history. Since the time of World War II we have not had any true leaders in this country. Someone once asked Gladstone, the great English jurist, what was the mark of a great statesman. He gave this answer: "A great statesman is a man who knows the direction God is going for the next fifty years." My friend, we certainly have not had leaders like that. As a result, we have missed a great opportunity as a nation for leadership in the world, and the great middle class of our nation has been corrupted. We are headed down, just as England went down, and just as Judah went down. We have refused to listen to the Word of God.

CHAPTER 29

THEME: Message of hope to first delegation of captives

JEREMIAH'S LETTER OF ENCOURAGEMENT

Now these are the words of the letter that Jeremiah the prophet sent from Jerusalem unto the residue of the elders which were carried away captives, and to the priests, and to the prophets, and to all the people whom Nebuchadnezzar had carried away captive from Jerusalem to Babylon [Jer. 29:1].

Chapter 29 records Jeremiah's letter to the people who had been taken into captivity when Jehoiachin was king (see 2 Kings 24:10–16). The complete captivity of Judah came eleven years later (2 Kings 25:1–7).

This is God's instruction to them:

Thus saith the LORD of hosts, the God of Israel, unto all that are carried away captives, whom I have caused to be carried away from Jerusalem unto Babylon;

Build ye houses, and dwell in them; and plant gardens, and eat the fruit of them;

Take ye wives, and beget sons and daughters; and take wives for your sons, and give your daughters to husbands, that they may bear sons and daughters; that ye may be increased there, and not diminished [Jer. 29:4–6].

That is, settle down in Babylon. Don't think you will be released any moment. Go ahead and plan for your future—get married and establish homes, because you are going to be there a long time.

> And seek the peace of the city whither I have caused you
> to be carried away captives, and pray unto the LORD for
> it: for in the peace thereof shall ye have peace [Jer. 29:7].

"Seek the peace of the city" in which you are living, and pray for it.
They were not to rebel or instigate revolt. They were to settle down
and be law-abiding citizens.

> For thus saith the LORD, That after seventy years be ac-
> complished at Babylon I will visit you, and perform my
> good word toward you, in causing you to return to this
> place [Jer. 29:10].

God tells them the exact number of years they will be in captivity, then
assures them that He has not forsaken them but will restore them to
their homeland.

LIES OF THE FALSE PROPHETS

There were false prophets in Babylon who refused to accept Jeremiah's letter as a message from God. They wrote letters to Jerusalem
claiming that God had appointed a new priest and that Jeremiah was
to be silenced.

> Then came the word of the LORD unto Jeremiah, saying,

> Send to all them of the captivity, saying, Thus saith the
> LORD concerning Shemaiah the Nehelamite; Because
> that Shemaiah hath prophesied unto you, and I sent him
> not, and he caused you to trust in a lie:

> Therefore thus saith the LORD; Behold, I will punish
> Shemaiah the Nehelamite, and his seed: he shall not
> have a man to dwell among this people; neither shall he
> behold the good that I will do for my people, saith the
> LORD; because he hath taught rebellion against the LORD
> [Jer. 29:30–32].

Of course, God pronounces a judgment against these false prophets.

God speaks very impressively in history. He has told Judah that what is happening to them is happening because of their sin. He will always judge sin. God has not changed. Many people would like to think that the God of the New Testament is different from the God of the Old Testament. He is the same person; He hasn't changed one bit. He hasn't grown old. He hasn't even learned anything new. He is the same God.

Not only has God spoken in history, but He has spoken in His Word. Listen to Simon Peter: "Knowing this first, that no prophecy of the scripture is of any private interpretation" (2 Pet. 1:20). "Knowing this first"—this is primary stuff, something we should learn in the first grade. There are two ways this verse has been understood which are incorrect. One is that when you study prophecy, you need to consider the whole of prophecy; you cannot take one prophecy by itself and study it to the exclusion of others. That is a true statement, but it is not what this passage is teaching. Then there are those who say you have no right to interpret prophecy on your own. Well, that not only takes away the freedom of the first amendment from me, but it also removes the free will that God gave to me. This is not what Peter is saying. He is not speaking at all about the end result of God's revelation; what he is talking about is the *origin* of it. No writing of Scripture was of private interpretation at its origin. The prophets who wrote and spoke in olden times are not giving you the result of their observations. They are speaking what *God* told them to speak.

When you and I approach the Word of God, we must come to the place where we are ready to lie in the dust. I do not mean to simply acknowledge that we are nothing, that we are sinners; but we must be willing to lay into the dust our opinions, our self-will, and our own viewpoints—to put it all down and listen to what *God* has to say. This was the problem with the priests and prophets and princes in Jeremiah's day. It is our problem today. Every man has his own little viewpoint, is doing his own little thing, carrying his own little placard of protest—and he's doing it out of limited knowledge.

God has all knowledge—He has all the facts, knows all the background. It is unbelievable that some people presume to sit in judgment of Him. Little man stands up and says, "Lord, if You're up there—and I'm not sure You are; I'm pretty hard to convince because I have a giant intellect, and my intellect says You may not even be up there—but if You're up there, I just want to say that You are *wrong*." Oh, my friend, what arrogance! If a little, old ant were to crawl into my house and onto my chair and look at me and say, "Look, I don't like the way you built this house; I don't like the way you plant flowers and trees around here; and I don't like what you eat," do you know what I would do to that ant? I would flick him off my chair and *step* on him. That would be the end of that little ant! But God is so gracious to man. He doesn't step on us. He has given us a second chance.

CHAPTER 30

THEME: The coming Great Tribulation

Chapters 30—39 form the fourth major section of the Book of Jeremiah, and they contain prophecies concerning the future of the twelve tribes of Israel and the near captivity of Judah. The prophecies in this section are not in chronological order.

The message in these chapters comes from Jeremiah to Judah in the darkest days she has ever had. It never got so dark that he didn't have a wonderful message of encouragement, however.

This is the situation: the army of Nebuchadnezzar is outside the walls of the city of Jerusalem, and they mean business. This time Nebuchadnezzar will destroy the city and burn the temple. Jeremiah has been arrested and shut up in the courtyard. Literally, he is in jail. It has been seven years since he had his conflict with the false prophets. Events have moved along rather quietly, but every day reveals the accuracy of Jeremiah's message. The false prophet Hananiah had said that the power of Babylon would be broken within two years. Seven years have gone by, and Nebuchadnezzar is outside the city wall. His power is not going to be broken; instead *he* is about to break Jerusalem. The vessels of the Lord's house are not going to be restored to the temple. Jeconiah will not be returned to the city. Things have gone from bad to worse. They are out of the frying pan into the fire. The life of the nation of Judah has gone down. With Jerusalem already under the shadow of Babylon, God's prophet is held captive by the rebellious spirit of a sinning nation which refuses to hear the Word of the Lord.

Can any hour be darker? Can any circumstances be more calculated to fill the heart with despair? Yet it is at this time that the prophetic note of Jeremiah's message goes all the way from the basement to the top floor of the Empire State Building. He is no longer singing low bass; now he's going to sing high tenor, if you please. He is going to reach the heights. He has come all the way through darkness into the light. The night cometh, but also the morning is coming.

The word that came to Jeremiah from the LORD, saying,

Thus speaketh the LORD God of Israel, saying, Write thee all the words that I have spoken unto thee in a book [Jer. 30:1–2].

He is *writing* his prophecy now. After all, he's in jail; he won't be in the pulpit on Sunday morning.

For, lo, the days come, saith the LORD, that I will bring again the captivity of my people Israel and Judah, saith the LORD: and I will cause them to return to the land that I gave to their fathers, and they shall possess it.

And these are the words that the LORD spake concerning Israel and concerning Judah.

For thus saith the LORD; We have heard a voice of trembling, of fear, and not of peace [Jer. 30:3–5].

Believe me, the people had gotten the message from Jeremiah that there would be no peace. The false prophets had said, "Peace, peace," and there was none.

Ask ye now, and see whether a man doth travail with child? wherefore do I see every man with his hands on his loins, as a woman in travail, and all faces are turned into paleness?

Alas! for that day is great, so that none is like it: it is even the time of Jacob's trouble; but he shall be saved out of it [Jer. 30:6–7].

Jeremiah sees the great Day of the Lord coming of which the other prophets, including Isaiah, also spoke. They said it is to be a day of darkness and not of light, that the people will go through the night of the Great Tribulation period before they will see the brightness of day. In effect God is saying, "You haven't seen anything yet. The Great

Tribulation period will be far worse than what you are going through now."

THE COMING KINGDOM

For it shall come to pass in that day, saith the LORD of hosts, that I will break his yoke from off thy neck, and will burst thy bonds, and strangers shall no more serve themselves of him:

But they shall serve the LORD their God, and David their king, whom I will raise up unto them [Jer. 30:8–9].

Out of that awful time of trouble, the people of Israel will return to the land. David will be raised from the dead and will rule over them as they enter the Kingdom Age.

Thus saith the LORD; Behold, I will bring again the captivity of Jacob's tents, and have mercy on his dwelling-places; and the city shall be builded upon her own heap, and the palace shall remain after the manner thereof [Jer. 30:18].

This is the sure promise of the Lord. When will these things take place?—

The fierce anger of the LORD shall not return, until he have done it, and until he have performed the intents of his heart: in the latter days ye shall consider it [Jer. 30:24].

"In the latter days"—this is a prophecy which is to be fulfilled in the future. It refers to the Kingdom Age which is, of course, still future in our day.

CHAPTER 31

Chapters 30 through 33 constitute one very bright and encouraging song. Up to this point Jeremiah's emphasis has been upon judgment, but his message now is in sharp contrast to that. E. W. Hengstenburg calls these chapters "the triumphal hymn of Israel's salvation." They were written at the darkest moment in the history of Judah.

As the last king of Judah, Zedekiah corresponds to Hoshea who was the final ruler of the northern kingdom of Israel. But, of course, the northern kingdom of Israel has long since departed and gone into captivity. At this moment Nebuchadnezzar's army is outside the wall of Jerusalem, ready to destroy the city and burn the temple. The promises of the false prophets have been proven false. Seven years earlier Hananiah had said that Babylon would be broken within two years. But Nebuchadnezzar is not broken; he is alive—too much alive for the people of Judah.

Jeremiah's message is a message of encouragement. In chapter 30 he spoke of the Day of the Lord opening with the Great Tribulation period. In verse 7 of that chapter he called it "the time of Jacob's trouble." But beyond the Great Tribulation is coming the restoration of the land and the return of the people to it.

I have labeled chapter 31 "the 'I will' chapter," because "I will" occurs fifteen times, and the One who says it is none other than God. When God says "I will" fifteen times, He is telling us what *He* is going to do.

> **At the same time, saith the LORD, will I be the God of all the families of Israel, and they shall be my people [Jer. 31:1].**

This prophecy has not yet been fulfilled; that time has not come. The present return of Israel to the land cannot be interpreted as being the fulfillment of this prophecy—because they have not returned to God. I am told there is real persecution of Christians in that land today. They talk about religious freedom, but it does not really exist. The people have returned to the land, but they have not returned to the LORD.

> **Thus saith the LORD, The people which were left of the sword found grace in the wilderness; even Israel, when I went to cause him to rest.**

> **The LORD hath appeared of old unto me, saying, Yea, I have loved thee with an everlasting love: therefore with lovingkindness have I drawn thee [Jer. 31:2–3].**

We have here the reason God is going to restore the people to the land. I believe with all my heart that God intends to restore the nation Israel to that land in His own time and in His own plan and in His own purpose. The basis for that is given right here: "I have loved thee with an everlasting love." This verse ranks high among the many favorite statements in the Word of God.

There are those who will ask, "*How* can God love these people?" That is a good question, but let's widen it out just a little and ask, "How can God love *us* today?" He has said, ". . . God so loved the world . . ." (John 3:16). Not only does God love Israel, He loves the world—He loves you and me. It is easy to point a finger at the Jews and be critical of them, but God says, "I have loved thee [Israel] with an everlasting love." There is nothing you can do with that—God has said it. Instead of pointing the finger at others, we need to turn it around and point at ourselves. In God's sight we are as great sinners as anyone who is still unbelieving. It took the death of Christ to provide a redemption for you and me. Don't limit it to a few and say, "How can God love *them*?" My friend, how can God love *me*? How can God love *you*? We should be amazed that He loved any of us.

Frederick W. Faber has expressed this very well in a song:

> How Thou canst think so well of us
> Yet be the God Thou art,

Is darkness to my intellect
But sunshine to my heart.

"I have loved thee with an everlasting love." "Everlasting"—I must confess that I know very little about the meaning of that word. I once asked a little boy, "How long is *everlasting* and how long is *never?*" He simply answered, "I reckon it's a pretty long time."

"Love"—what is love, by the way? The only explanation I have for why God loves us is that it is not because of anything He sees in us but it is *because of who He is*. He finds the explanation in Himself. John wrote "Herein is love, not that we loved God, but that he loved us . . ." (1 John 4:10). Now that is love. Cramer commented on what John said: "The love of God toward us comes from love, and has no other cause above or beside itself, but is in God, and remains in God, so that Christ Who is in God is its Centre" (in *Studies in the Prophecy of Jeremiah*, G. Campbell Morgan, p. 167). God loves you and me, my friend, and I really cannot tell you why.

Again, let me quote Faber:

Yet Thou dost think so well of us,
Because of what Thou art;
Thy love illumines our intellect,
Yet fills with fear our heart.

I am overwhelmed by the love of God. If He were to change His mind tomorrow, I would be eternally lost and so would you. But He says His love is everlasting, and that's a pretty long time.

I have a great many amillennial friends who believe that God is through with the nation Israel. May I say to you, if He's through with Israel, then He's through with you and He's through with me. But He says, "I have loved you with an everlasting love." It doesn't make any difference what you and I think—God is not through with Israel.

Behold, I will bring them from the north country, and gather them from the coasts of the earth, and with them

**the blind and the lame, the woman with child and her
that travaileth with child together: a great company
shall return thither [Jer. 31:8].**

It is going to be such a big undertaking to bring the people back to the
land you might think that He would leave the blind and the lame behind and just bring the best physical specimens. God says, "Nothing
of the kind. I am going to bring them all back."

**They shall come with weeping, and with supplications
will I lead them: I will cause them to walk by the rivers
of waters in a straight way, wherein they shall not stum-
ble: for I am a father to Israel, and Ephraim is my firstborn [Jer. 31:9].**

"I am a father to Israel, and Ephraim is my firstborn." God never said
that He was Father to any individual Israelite. He said, "Moses, My
servant" (see Josh. 1:2), and "David, My servant" (see Ps. 89:3). But
when He speaks of the whole nation as a corporate body, God says, "I
am a father to Israel" (see Exod. 4:22).

**Hear the word of the LORD, O ye nations, and declare it
in the isles afar off, and say, He that scattered Israel will
gather him, and keep him, as a shepherd doth his flock
[Jer. 31:10].**

I am grateful that the Lord has given to me a radio ministry that
reaches around the world each day. I am delighted that I can say what
God also says, that I want the isles of the earth to hear the message. I
want all mankind to hear that He scattered Israel. It was a judgment
upon them, but He loves them with an everlasting love, and He is
going to bring them back to the land.

He loved Israel and He judged them. This is a bittersweet message.
All through Jeremiah you have a note of joy, but you also have a note of
sorrow. It is like the Chinese dishes that are called "sweet and sour."

God judged Israel, but He also said, "He that scattered Israel will gather him, and keep him, as a shepherd doth his flock." And a shepherd really watches over his flock.

God is not through saying what He *will* do:

> **Then shall the virgin rejoice in the dance, both young men and old together: for I will turn their mourning into joy, and will comfort them, and make them rejoice from their sorrow.**

> **And I will satiate the soul of the priests with fatness, and my people shall be satisfied with my goodness, saith the LORD [Jer. 31:13–14].**

I don't know about you, but this makes me feel like saying, "Hallelujah!" and throwing my hat in the air. This is what *God* says He is going to do for *Israel*; let's allow Him to say it, for it's what He wants to do.

Yet Israel's immediate condition was tragic. They had rebelled against God, and they were backslidden.

> **How long wilt thou go about, O thou backsliding daughter? for the LORD hath created a new thing in the earth, A woman shall compass a man [Jer. 31:22].**

There are those who believe that this verse refers to the virgin birth of Jesus Christ, and I see no reason to rule that out.

Beginning at verse 31 we have the new covenant that God intends to make with Israel—all twelve tribes. And if you think that ten of the tribes are lost, God does not. He is going to make this covenant with all twelve tribes.

> **Behold, the days come, saith the LORD, that I will make a new covenant with the house of Israel, and with the house of Judah:**

Not according to the covenant that I made with their fathers in the day that I took them by the hand to bring them out of the land of Egypt; which my covenant they brake, although I was an husband unto them, saith the LORD:

But this shall be the covenant that I will make with the house of Israel; After those days, saith the LORD, I will put my law in their inward parts, and write it in their hearts; and will be their God, and they shall be my people [Jer. 31:31–33].

This new covenant is going to be different from the one given to Moses at Mount Sinai. The grand distinction is that it will be engraved upon the hearts of the people and not upon cold tables of stone.

And they shall teach no more every man his neighbour, and every man his brother, saying, Know the LORD: for they shall all know me, from the least of them unto the greatest of them, saith the LORD: for I will forgive their iniquity, and I will remember their sin no more [Jer. 31:34].

Their sins will be forgiven.

Notice how God confirms this covenant to Israel:

Thus saith the LORD, which giveth the sun for a light by day, and the ordinances of the moon and of the stars for a light by night, which divideth the sea when the waves thereof roar; The LORD of hosts is his name:

If those ordinances depart from before me, saith the LORD, then the seed of Israel also shall cease from being a nation before me for ever [Jer. 31:35–36].

This covenant will never be changed or abrogated. Just as we cannot change the course of the moon or pull it out of the sky, so His covenant with Israel cannot be changed. On a trip to the moon we brought back two hundred pounds of rock. If we kept doing that for a few million years, maybe we would eventually move the whole thing to earth— but I don't think we're going to do that! God says this is an everlasting covenant that He will make with them.

CHAPTERS 32 AND 33

THEME: *Imprisoned Jeremiah buys real estate; coming Kingdom as promised to David*

In chapter 32 Jeremiah is in prison, and Jerusalem is under siege by Nebuchadnezzar; yet Jeremiah buys a piece of real estate in Anathoth!

> **The word that came to Jeremiah from the Lord in the tenth year of Zedekiah king of Judah, which was the eighteenth year of Nebuchadrezzar.**
>
> **For then the king of Babylon's army besieged Jerusalem: and Jeremiah the prophet was shut up in the court of the prison, which was in the king of Judah's house [Jer. 32:1–2].**

Notice how Jeremiah pinpoints the time: it was "the tenth year of Zedekiah," the year Nebuchadnezzar breached the walls of Jerusalem and destroyed it. It was a dark day indeed.

> **Behold, Hanameel the son of Shallum thine uncle shall come unto thee, saying, Buy thee my field that is in Anathoth: for the right of redemption is thine to buy it [Jer. 32:7].**

The Lord told Jeremiah that he would have the opportunity to buy a piece of land from his relative, Hanameel.

> **And I bought the field of Hanameel my uncle's son, that was in Anathoth, and weighed him the money, even seventeen shekels of silver [Jer. 32:9].**

At the darkest hour in Judah's history, Jeremiah buys real estate—this was the time to be *selling* real estate! I imagine that the real estate men in Jerusalem and the surrounding country were dumping all the real estate they possibly could. Why did Jeremiah buy this piece of land at this time? It was to show the people he believed God when He said that they were going to return to the land. This is very remarkable.

But Jeremiah had a question which was too hard for him to answer, and in the following verses he brings this question to the Lord in prayer.

> **Now when I had delivered the evidence of the purchase unto Baruch the son of Neriah, I prayed unto the LORD, saying,**
>
> **Ah Lord God! behold, thou hast made the heaven and the earth by thy great power and stretched out arm, and there is nothing too hard for thee [Jer. 32:16–17].**

Jeremiah's question is too hard for him to answer, but it is not too hard for God.

In verses 18 through 23, Jeremiah recounts the way the Lord has protected and provided for Israel down through her history, but now the situation is very grave.

> **Behold the mounts, they are come unto the city to take it; and the city is given into the hand of the Chaldeans, that fight against it, because of the sword, and of the famine, and of the pestilence: and what thou hast spoken is come to pass; and, behold, thou seest it.**
>
> **And thou hast said unto me, O Lord GOD, Buy thee the field for money, and take witnesses; for the city is given into the hand of the Chaldeans [Jer. 32:24–25].**

Jeremiah is no hypocrite. He trusts the God who made heaven and earth, the God who had so wonderfully cared for Israel. But now the Chaldeans are right outside the city and are going to take it; yet God told Jeremiah to buy a field. He obeyed, but it didn't make good sense to him. So he brings his question to the Lord.

My friend, there is nothing wrong with asking why. If you have a doubt or a question, talk to the Lord about it. That is what He wants us to do. Just don't put up this pious hypocritical front that we sometimes see. While he says he trusts the Lord, he is crying and complaining and asking why. Let's be honest like Jeremiah. He obeyed the Lord, but he admitted his doubts, taking them to the Lord in prayer.

God answers Jeremiah's prayer in verses 26 through 44.

> **Then came the word of the LORD unto Jeremiah, saying,**
>
> **Behold, I am the LORD, the God of all flesh: is there any thing too hard for me? [Jer. 32:26–27].**

The Lord begins by putting down the axiom that nothing is too hard for Him.

> **And now therefore thus saith the LORD, the God of Israel, concerning this city, whereof ye say, It shall be delivered into the hand of the king of Babylon by the sword, and by the famine, and by the pestilence;**
>
> **Behold, I will gather them out of all countries, whither I have driven them in mine anger, and in my fury, and in great wrath; and I will bring them again unto this place, and I will cause them to dwell safely:**
>
> **And they shall be my people, and I will be their God:**
>
> **And I will give them one heart, and one way, that they may fear me for ever, for the good of them, and of their children after them:**
>
> **And I will make an everlasting covenant with them, that I will not turn away from them, to do them good; but I will put my fear in their hearts, that they shall not depart from me [Jer. 32:36–40].**

God is delivering the city over to the Chaldeans, and in His own time He will deliver the city *from* the Chaldeans.

> **Yea, I will rejoice over them to do them good, and I will plant them in this land assuredly with my whole heart and with my whole soul.**
>
> **For thus saith the LORD; Like as I have brought all this great evil upon this people, so I will bring upon them all the good that I have promised them [Jer. 32:41–42].**

Now Jehovah is delivering Judah unto judgment. In a future day, He will deliver them in mercy—this is His promise.

When we go to God and let Him know how we feel, He will encourage our hearts as He did for Jeremiah. Oh, my friend, He wants you to come to Him.

The day is very dark for Judah, but God allows Jeremiah to look down through the tunnel to where light can be seen at the other end. In chapter 33 God confirms and reaffirms the covenant that He made with David. There is a day coming when He will restore the people to the land of Israel and to fellowship with Himself.

> **Moreover the word of the LORD came unto Jeremiah the second time, while he was yet shut up in the court of the prison, saying [Jer. 33:1].**

Jeremiah is still in jail, you see.

> **Thus saith the LORD the maker thereof, the LORD that formed it, to establish it; the LORD is his name;**
>
> **Call unto me, and I will answer thee, and shew thee great and mighty things, which thou knowest not [Jer. 33:2–3].**

This last verse I have heard quoted frequently at testimony meetings. It is a very wonderful verse, but I think it is more meaningful if it is remembered in the context of this chapter. Despite the fact that he is in prison, this man was told by God to buy a piece of real estate. Jeremiah acted by faith and bought the real estate, but he has a great many questions in his mind. Why was God permitting Judah to go into captivity? Frankly, I think it is an example of great faith when a believer has these moments of doubt. Someone will ask how that can be. My friend, if you are walking with God and are in fellowship with Him, He is so wonderful and He does such wonderful things that there will be times when you do not understand what He is doing. Our question is bound to be, "Why are You doing this?" Don't you have questions like that?

I have had questions like that. I remember one evening going to the hospital to see my wife and our firstborn baby. The nurse said to me, "The doctor wants to speak to you," and she looked very serious. The doctor said to me, "The little baby died." He hadn't told my wife, so he and I went in and told her and we wept together. I walked out (I never shall forget) to an open-air porch there at the hospital. It was summertime, and I looked up at the heavens and the stars. I had a question. Do you know what that question was? Why? Why? I still look up and ask that same question. Over the years I have learned to put my hand in His and just keep walking in the dark. Many times I talk this over with Him, and I tell Him about my doubts, but I also tell Him that I trust Him. I'm glad that Jeremiah was that kind of a man. And there are other men in Scripture who also had questions they asked God. In the Book of Habakkuk, we find that Habakkuk had a lot of questions. In fact, his book is just a great big "WHY?" Jonah also had some questions to ask the Lord. My friend, such questions are not a revelation of a lack of faith, but it is hypocrisy to pretend that we have accepted God's ways and are walking in complete submission to Him when actually we are having questions deep inside. I believe that God wants us to be completely honest with Him above everything else. And this is His promise to us: "Call unto me, and I will answer thee, and shew thee great and mighty things, which thou knowest not."

Now God is going to reaffirm the covenant He made with David in 2 Samuel 7. He made a covenant with David that there would be one to sit on his throne forever. This covenant became the theme song of every prophet, so much so that they all sound like a stuck record. They all refer back to this covenant and rest upon it. Listen to Jeremiah:

> Behold, the days come, saith the LORD, that I will perform that good thing which I have promised unto the house of Israel and to the house of Judah.
>
> In those days, and at that time, will I cause the Branch of righteousness to grow up unto David; and he shall execute judgment and righteousness in the land [Jer. 33:14–15].

"In those days" refers to the day which is coming, the Day of the Lord.

"The Branch of righteousness to grow up unto David." There hasn't been a righteous branch so far except One, the One who was born in Bethlehem.

"He shall execute judgment and righteousness in the land." We haven't had any ruler like that yet.

> In those days shall Judah be saved, and Jerusalem shall dwell safely: and this is the name wherewith she shall be called, The LORD our righteousness [Jer. 33:16].

"The LORD our righteousness" in the Hebrew is *Jehovah-tsidkenu*. If you and I have any righteousness it is in Jesus Christ. *He* is our righteousness.

> For thus saith the LORD; David shall never want a man to sit upon the throne of the house of Israel [Jer. 33:17].

Where do you think this man is today? There is not an Israelite on topside of the earth who can make the claim to David's throne. The One who has that claim is sitting at God's right hand as the psalmist explained: "The LORD said unto my Lord, Sit thou at my right hand, until I make thine enemies thy footstool" (Ps. 110:1). God is busy calling out a people to His name, getting things ready to put His Son on the throne of this universe.

> **And the word of the LORD came unto Jeremiah, saying,**
>
> **Thus saith the LORD; If ye can break my covenant of the day, and my covenant of the night, and that there should not be day and night in their season;**
>
> **Then may also my covenant be broken with David my servant, that he should not have a son to reign upon his throne; and with the Levites the priests, my ministers.**
>
> **As the host of heaven cannot be numbered, neither the sand of the sea measured: so will I multiply the seed of David my servant, and the Levites that minister unto me [Jer. 33:19–22].**

At the time this prophecy was given, Zedekiah was on the throne of Judah. He was as corrupt as any man ever was. Nebuchadnezzar will put out his eyes and carry him into captivity. You would think that this would put an end to the line of David. It would end the line of any other nation, I can assure you. There is no one around to claim the throne of the king of Babylon. There is no one to take Alexander the Great's place. There is no pharaoh in Egypt today. But there is One in David's line who can claim his throne. God says that He intends to put Him on the throne of this universe someday. This is a great prophecy and one which is very difficult to ignore or to spiritualize. I think God means exactly what He says.

CHAPTERS 34—36

THEME: Zedekiah's captivity foretold; Rechabites obey
God and Jehoiakim destroys Word of God

The word which came unto Jeremiah from the Lord,
when Nebuchadnezzar king of Babylon, and all his
army, and all the kingdoms of the earth of his dominion,
and all the people, fought against Jerusalem, and
against all the cities thereof, saying,

Thus saith the Lord, the God of Israel; Go and speak to
Zedekiah king of Judah, and tell him, Thus saith the
Lord; Behold, I will give this city into the hand of the
king of Babylon, and he shall burn it with fire:

And thou shalt not escape out of his hand, but shalt
surely be taken, and delivered into his hand; and thine
eyes shall behold the eyes of the king of Babylon, and he
shall speak with thee mouth to mouth, and thou shalt go
to Babylon.

Yet hear the word of the Lord, O Zedekiah king of Judah; Thus saith the Lord of thee, Thou shalt not die by
the sword:

But thou shalt die in peace: and with the burnings of thy
fathers, the former kings which were before thee, so
shall they burn odours for thee; and they will lament
thee, saying, Ah lord! for I have pronounced the word,
saith the Lord [Jer. 34:1–5].

Jeremiah is to prophesy that the city of Jerusalem is to be burned
with fire by the king of Babylon and that Zedekiah himself will be
taken captive.

This is the word that came unto Jeremiah from the LORD, after that the king Zedekiah had made a covenant with all the people which were at Jerusalem, to proclaim liberty unto them;

That every man should let his manservant, and every man his maidservant, being an Hebrew or an Hebrewess, go free; that none should serve himself of them, to wit, of a Jew his brother [Jer. 34:8-9].

Zedekiah made an agreement with the people that all the Hebrew servants should be set free.

And ye were now turned, and had done right in my sight, in proclaiming liberty every man to his neighbour; and ye had made a covenant before me in the house which is called by my name:

But ye turned and polluted my name, and caused every man his servant, and every man his handmaid, whom ye had set at liberty at their pleasure, to return, and brought them into subjection, to be unto you for servants and for handmaids [Jer. 34:15-16].

The Lord said that the covenant was "right in my sight" (see Exod. 21:2).

But Zedekiah did not make good on his covenant, and the Lord said of him, "ye turned and polluted my name." In other words, Zedekiah profaned the name of God. By truly granting liberty to the people, Zedekiah, as king of Judah, could have demonstrated to the world that he was different, that he served the living and true God. But it was just a pretense; he didn't make good on his promise. He not only brought himself into disrepute, but he profaned the name of God.

It is the *life* of the child of God that the world will always look at. God's name and the furtherance of His Word is hurt more by those who profess to know Him than by all the godless professors in our colleges today. The lives of those who name the name of Christ can hurt His cause more than those who are unbelieving. God says, "You have polluted My name; you have profaned My name."

> **The princes of Judah, and the princes of Jerusalem, the eunuchs, and the priests, and all the people of the land, which passed between the parts of the calf;**

> **I will even give them into the hand of their enemies, and into the hand of them that seek their life: and their dead bodies shall be for meat unto the fowls of the heaven, and to the beasts of the earth.**

> **And Zedekiah king of Judah and his princes will I give into the hand of their enemies, and into the hand of them that seek their life, and into the hand of the king of Babylon's army, which are gone up from you [Jer. 34:19–21].**

"Which passed between the parts of the calf." This is the way men made a covenant or a contract in that day. They took a sacrifice and cut it in half, putting half of the animal on one side and half on the other. The men then went between and joined hands. This is also the way God made His covenant with Abraham. It is like going to the notary public in our day. Zedekiah, the princes, the priests, and the people had all violated God's covenant in not granting liberty to the servants, and therefore God pronounces this judgment upon them.

In chapter 35 we find the Rechabites who are part of the believing remnant, and they are in sharp contrast to the nation as a whole. God has given us this account to remind us that there has always been a remnant—He will never leave the world without a witness to Himself. Even in the darkest time in history the world will ever know—the Great Tribulation period which is yet future, when the 144,000 will have been forced underground—there will still be two witnesses who are going to stand for God. That is just the way God is going to have it. Even at the time when Satan is being allowed to run the whole show, God says, "I will keep two witnesses around, and they will be inviolate—you won't be able to touch them—until their mission has been accomplished."

> **The word which came unto Jeremiah from the LORD in the days of Jehoiakim the son of Josiah king of Judah, saying,**
>
> **Go unto the house of the Rechabites, and speak unto them, and bring them into the house of the LORD, into one of the chambers, and give them wine to drink [Jer. 35:1–2].**

The Lord tells Jeremiah to bring the Rechabites to the house of the Lord and give them wine to drink.

> **And I set before the sons of the house of the Rechabites pots full of wine, and cups, and I said unto them, Drink ye wine.**
>
> **But they said, We will drink no wine: for Jonadab the son of Rechab our father commanded us, saying, Ye shall drink no wine, neither ye, nor your sons for ever [Jer. 35:5–6].**

On the basis of a command that had been given to their family many years before, the Rechabites refuse the wine that Jeremiah gives to them.

> **Thus saith the LORD of hosts, the God of Israel; Go and tell the men of Judah and the inhabitants of Jerusalem, Will ye not receive instruction to hearken to my words? saith the LORD.**
>
> **The words of Jonadab the son of Rechab, that he commanded his sons not to drink wine, are performed; for unto this day they drink none, but obey their father's commandment: notwithstanding I have spoken unto**

you, rising early and speaking; but ye hearkened not unto me.

I have sent also unto you all my servants the prophets, rising up early and sending them, saying, Return ye now every man from his evil way, and amend your doings, and go not after other gods to serve them, and ye shall dwell in the land which I have given to you and to your fathers: but ye have not inclined your ear, nor hearkened unto me [Jer. 35:13–15].

God draws this sharp contrast between the Rechabites who faithfully obey the commands of their earthly father and the children of Judah who have failed to hearken to the commands of their loving heavenly Father. In the remainder of the chapter He goes on to pronounce judgment on the people of Judah and blessing upon the Rechabites.

Chapter 36 reveals the attitude which Jehoiakim had toward the Word of God and the messages God sent to him through His prophet, Jeremiah.

And it came to pass in the fourth year of Jehoiakim the son of Josiah king of Judah, that this word came unto Jeremiah from the LORD, saying,

Take thee a roll of a book, and write therein all the words that I have spoken unto thee against Israel, and against Judah, and against all the nations, from the day I spake unto thee, from the days of Josiah, even unto this day [Jer. 36:1–2].

God told Jeremiah to record all His words in a book; so Jeremiah dictated all of God's words to Baruch who wrote them down for him. Then Jeremiah commanded Baruch to take the roll into the house of the Lord and read it in the hearing of all the people. When the princes heard what had taken place, they sent for Baruch and had him read the roll in their presence.

> Then said the princes unto Baruch, Go, hide thee, thou and Jeremiah; and let no man know where ye be.
>
> And they went in to the king into the court, but they laid up the roll in the chamber of Elishama the scribe, and told all the words in the ears of the king.
>
> So the king sent Jehudi to fetch the roll: and he took it out of Elishama the scribe's chamber. And Jehudi read it in the ears of the king, and in the ears of all the princes which stood beside the king.
>
> Now the king sat in the winterhouse in the ninth month: and there was a fire on the hearth burning before him.
>
> And it came to pass, that when Jehudi had read three or four leaves, he cut it with the penknife, and cast it into the fire that was on the hearth, until all the roll was consumed in the fire that was on the hearth [Jer. 36:19–23].

That shows you what Jehoiakim thought of the Word of God: he took it and just flung it into the fire! He didn't care for it. He didn't accept it. He didn't believe it.

I am not impressed that the Bible is still the best seller of all books. Who is actually *reading* the Bible today? Ignoring the Bible is really no different from throwing it into the fire as Jehoiakim did. Here is a sad little jingle that someone sent to me that illustrates the condition in our country today:

> "Maw, I found an old, dusty thing high
>   upon the shelf. Just look!"
> "Why, that's a Bible. Tommy dear, be
>   careful. That's God's Book."
> "God's Book?" the young one said,
>   "Then, Maw, before we lose it
> We'd better send it back to God, 'cause
>   you know we never use it."

> **Yet they were not afraid, nor rent their garments, neither
> the king, nor any of his servants that heard all these
> words [Jer. 36:24].**

There was no fear or remorse because of what they had done.

If you think God is going to stop here because Jehoiakim has destroyed His Word, you are wrong.

> **Take thee again another roll, and write in it all the
> former words that were in the first roll, which Jeho-
> iakim the king of Judah hath burned [Jer. 36:28].**

God tells Jeremiah to write it all over again and to send a message to Jehoiakim:

> **Therefore thus saith the LORD of Jehoiakim king of Ju-
> dah; He shall have none to sit upon the throne of David:
> and his dead body shall be cast out in the day to the
> heat, and in the night to the frost [Jer. 36:30].**

This is exactly what happened to Jehoiakim. He has no one to sit upon the throne of David today. The Lord Jesus who does have claim to that throne did not come in his line. Mary was born in the line of Nathan, another son of David, and it is through her that the Lord Jesus has blood title to the throne of David. No one in the line of Jehoiakim will ever sit on that throne.

CHAPTERS 37—39

THEME: Word of God destroyed; Jeremiah imprisoned but then released; Judah begins captivity

We move now into a new section of the book which places the emphasis on the historical events. Jeremiah could be saying, "I told you so," but he is too much involved. He is crushed and broken by the message which he has had to give to the people and now by its fulfillment as the city that he loves is destroyed and the nation he loves goes into captivity. Jeremiah has been faithful in revealing God and acting as His witness. If you want to know how God feels about all that is taking place, look into the face of Jeremiah with the tears streaming down his cheeks.

Over thirty years of ministry have gone by for Jeremiah. We saw him start as a young man of about twenty years of age, a young priest who was called to be a prophet of God. Now he is in prison, and the army of the king of Babylon is outside the walls of Jerusalem. They have been there for a long siege of eighteen months duration. Jeremiah gives some of this history in chapter 52, and more is recorded in 2 Kings and in 2 Chronicles.

This is now the third and final time that Nebuchadnezzar has come down against Jerusalem. The other two times he had taken a certain number of the people captive and had placed Zedekiah on the throne as his vassal. Zedekiah wanted to get out from under the king of Babylon, so he made an overture to Pharaoh of Egypt. Pharaoh decided to come up to try to relieve Zedekiah. Of course, what he planned to do was to put Judah under the rule of Egypt. When Pharaoh came up to Jerusalem, the commanders of Nebuchadnezzar turned aside, and instead of besieging the city they withdrew. At this point it looked as if the prophecies of Jeremiah might be wrong. So God gave to Jeremiah this very strong word:

Thus saith the LORD, the God of Israel; Thus shall ye say to the king of Judah, that sent you unto me to inquire of

me; Behold, Pharaoh's army, which is come forth to help you, shall return to Egypt into their own land.

And the Chaldeans shall come again, and fight against this city, and take it, and burn it with fire.

Thus saith the LORD; Deceive not yourselves, saying, The Chaldeans shall surely depart from us: for they shall not depart.

For though ye had smitten the whole army of the Chaldeans that fight against you, and there remained but wounded men among them, yet should they rise up every man in his tent, and burn this city with fire [Jer. 37:7–10].

The destruction of Jerusalem was determined by God. Even though it looked as if Babylon's armies had been frightened away, they would be back.

There are five recorded imprisonments of the prophet. The imprisonment described in this chapter was due to the fact that Jeremiah had said to the king that he was not to make an alliance with Pharaoh but was to surrender to Babylon.

And it came to pass, that when the army of the Chaldeans was broken up from Jerusalem for fear of Pharaoh's army,

Then Jeremiah went forth out of Jerusalem to go into the land of Benjamin, to separate himself thence in the midst of the people [Jer. 37:11–12].

While the city is being relieved, Jeremiah comes out of Jerusalem to go up to his hometown of Anathoth. Now notice what happens—

And when he was in the gate of Benjamin, a captain of the ward was there, whose name was Irijah, the son of

Shelemiah, the son of Hananiah; and he took Jeremiah the prophet, saying, Thou fallest away to the Chaldeans [Jer. 37:13].

He made the accusation against Jeremiah that he was going over to the enemy.

Then said Jeremiah, It is false; I fall not away to the Chaldeans. But he hearkened not to him: so Irijah took Jeremiah, and brought him to the princes.

Wherefore the princes were wroth with Jeremiah, and smote him, and put him in prison in the house of Jonathan the scribe: for they had made that the prison [Jer. 37:14–15].

Poor Jeremiah was not only put in prison, but he was put in the dungeon—for how long, we are not told. The next verse says only that it was for "many days." This was a time of great suffering for Jeremiah, but God had not forgotten. He moved the king to call for him.

Then Zedekiah the king sent, and took him out: and the king asked him secretly in his house, and said, Is there any word from the LORD? And Jeremiah said, There is: for, said he, thou shalt be delivered into the hand of the king of Babylon [Jer. 37:17].

Then Jeremiah takes this occasion to plead for his life:

Therefore hear now, I pray thee, O my lord the king: let my supplication, I pray thee, be accepted before thee; that thou cause me not to return to the house of Jonathan the scribe, lest I die there [Jer. 37:20].

The king didn't release him, but at least he saved his life.

> Then Zedekiah the king commanded that they should
> commit Jeremiah into the court of the prison, and that
> they should give him daily a piece of bread out of the
> bakers' street, until all the bread in the city were spent.
> Thus Jeremiah remained in the court of the prison [Jer.
> 37:21].

Jeremiah will remain in prison now until the armies of Babylon take
the city of Jerusalem.

JEREMIAH NARROWLY ESCAPES DEATH

When we come to chapter 38, Jeremiah is still confined to the court
of the prison, and he faithfully relays God's Word to his people even
though his personal safety is endangered.

The princes of Judah consider him a traitor to his country and a
demoralizing influence among the people; so they get permission
from the king to silence Jeremiah by putting him in the dungeon.

> Then took they Jeremiah, and cast him into the dungeon
> of Malchiah the son of Hammelech, that was in the
> court of the prison: and they let down Jeremiah with
> cords. And in the dungeon there was no water, but mire:
> so Jeremiah sunk in the mire [Jer. 38:6].

Again God sent someone to his rescue (vv. 7–13). This is a thrill-
ing rescue—I hope you will read the text carefully. After this, Zedekiah the king secretly asked Jeremiah to tell him what the Lord was
saying to him now. And he promised to save Jeremiah from those who
were seeking his life.

> Then said Jeremiah unto Zedekiah, Thus saith the Lord,
> the God of hosts, the God of Israel; If thou wilt assur-
> edly go forth unto the king of Babylon's princes, then
> thy soul shall live, and this city shall not be burned with
> fire; and thou shalt live, and thine house [Jer. 38:17].

Again he said, "Surrender! You can't resist this man."

> But if thou wilt not go forth to the king of Babylon's princes, then shall this city be given into the hand of the Chaldeans, and they shall burn it with fire, and thou shalt not escape out of their hand.
>
> And Zedekiah the king said unto Jeremiah, I am afraid of the Jews that are fallen to the Chaldeans, lest they deliver me into their hand, and they mock me.
>
> But Jeremiah said, They shall not deliver thee. Obey, I beseech thee, the voice of the LORD, which I speak unto thee: so it shall be well unto thee, and thy soul shall live [Jer. 38:18–20].

Jeremiah is pleading with Zedekiah to surrender to save his own life and the life of his people. His refusal to follow the course of action which Jeremiah presents will doom his nation.

Zedekiah is a coward at heart. He tries to make peace with everybody and to please everybody. He is a typical politician. As a result, he pleases nobody.

> But if thou refuse to go forth, this is the word that the LORD hath shewed me:
>
> And, behold, all the women that are left in the king of Judah's house shall be brought forth to the king of Babylon's princes, and those women shall say, Thy friends have set thee on, and have prevailed against thee: thy feet are sunk in the mire, and they are turned away back [Jer. 38:21–22].

A study of this period of Judah's history reveals that womanhood was pretty much corrupt. When womanhood becomes corrupt in any nation, there is very little hope for it on the moral plane. This is the picture here.

The foolish king will not heed the warning of God through Jeremiah. Instead he will continue to listen to the optimistic forecast of the false prophets.

In chapter 39 the awful carnage that Jeremiah had been predicting takes place.

> **In the ninth year of Zedekiah king of Judah, in the tenth month, came Nebuchadrezzar king of Babylon and all his army against Jerusalem, and they besieged it.**
>
> **And in the eleventh year of Zedekiah, in the fourth month, the ninth day of the month, the city was broken up [Jer. 39:1-2].**

In the following verses we see the fall of Jerusalem. King Zedekiah and the army attempt to escape from the city by night, but the army of Babylon overtakes them and delivers them to Nebuchadnezzar their king.

> **Then the king of Babylon slew the sons of Zedekiah in Riblah before his eyes: also the king of Babylon slew all the nobles of Judah.**
>
> **Moreover he put out Zedekiah's eyes, and bound him with chains, to carry him to Babylon [Jer. 39:6-7].**

The last chapter of the Book of Jeremiah gives a view of this horrible time in retrospect. It mentions the things that evidently were impressed upon the mind of Jeremiah. There he mentions again the fact that the king of Babylon killed the sons of Zedekiah before his eyes, then blinded Zedekiah.

JEREMIAH RELEASED BY THE ENEMY

It is interesting to note that Nebuchadnezzar instructed his men to release Jeremiah from prison and to treat him well.

Take him, and look well to him, and do him no harm; but do unto him even as he shall say unto thee [Jer. 39:12].

God was still taking care of His faithful prophet.

Even they sent, and took Jeremiah out of the court of the prison, and committed him unto Gedaliah the son of Ahikam the son of Shaphan, that he should carry him home: so he dwelt among the people [Jer. 39:14].

This begins that period which our Lord called "the times of the Gentiles." He said, ". . . and Jerusalem shall be trodden down of the Gentiles, until the times of the Gentiles be fulfilled" (Luke 21:24). I insist that Gentiles are still treading down Jerusalem. The Gentiles are still actually in control, and Israel doesn't really control the holy places in that land—except the Wailing Wall where they can go and weep. The words of the Lord Jesus are still true.

It is difficult for our contemporary generation to accept the fact of the judgment of God—that the judgment of God can come upon a nation, upon a family, upon an individual. Jeremiah had proclaimed the Word of Jehovah for forty years. He had denounced the sins of the people and had called these people to repentance. God had been very patient with them, and His very patience had deceived them. It enabled the false prophets to say, "See, the words of Jeremiah have not come to pass." But now his words have come to pass, and it is too late. God is patient with people and will let them go on and on until there comes a time when there is no remedy. Judah is an outstanding example of this. God pleaded with them through Jeremiah right up to the last moment. They spurned God, and the day finally came when Nebuchadnezzar leveled the city.

Humanity—all of mankind—does not like to hear that God is going to judge. It is hard for people to believe that God ever gets angry. Some folk try to say that it is the God of the Old Testament who is a God of wrath, that the New Testament gives a different picture of God.

May I say to you there is more said about divine wrath and anger in the New Testament than there is in the Old. Read Matthew 23 and listen to the frightful things said by the gentle Jesus: "Woe unto you, scribes and Pharisees, hypocrites. . . . Ye serpents, ye generation of vipers, how can ye escape the damnation of hell?" (Matt. 23:29, 33). Then read the Book of Revelation where the bowls of the wrath of God are poured out. There is nothing to equal that in the Old Testament. Don't try to say that the God of the Old Testament is a God of wrath and the God of the New Testament is a God of love. I tell you that He is always in every age both the God of love and the God of wrath. God punishes sin. You will always find divine judgment and divine mercy side by side. The throne of God is a throne of grace, a place to find mercy and help, but that very same throne will judge this earth someday. Man today finds this very difficult to understand.

God's laws are inexorable, and judgment is the penalty for disobedience of those laws. It seems so difficult for men to understand this in the moral and spiritual sphere when it is perfectly obvious in the natural sphere. If you don't believe that is true, I suggest you go to Yosemite Valley where there is a sheer surface of a rock several thousand feet high called El Capitan. If you step off El Capitan, you know what will happen. In nature there are certain laws that are inexorable. If you obey them, you may live; if you disobey them, you will die.

We think it is such a wonderful feat for men to walk on the moon, and it is. But do you realize that it was possible only because those men were *obeying* all the natural laws of God? They didn't *dare* break them. When they started for the moon, they didn't aim for the moon; they aimed for the position the moon would be in when they would arrive there. They knew exactly where it would be at the time of their arrival because the movements of this universe are governed by laws. If those fellows had ignored those laws of space and movement, they would have been lost out there in space and would be dead.

Human history should teach us the same lesson. All we need to do is walk down through the corridor of time and look at the debris and the ashes and the wreckage of the great civilizations of this world. They testify that God is a God of vengeance, a God of punishment, a God of judgment. When nations turned from high ideals and lofty moral planes to base ideals, they went down and passed off the stage of human history. It is about time for the intellectuals in this country to begin to read history correctly and to see that God moves in human history.

Now I admit that I feel like a square for saying this, but I don't feel bad about it because Jeremiah was also a square in his day. From our perspective in the twentieth century we can see that the king, old Zedekiah, was *pigheaded!* And the intellectuals, the sophisticates, the ones who had ruled God out, were *stupid!* So I don't mind being called an intellectual obscurantist, because I find that I am in very good company. I am going to be like Jeremiah was—just a man who believes God.

CHAPTERS 40—42

THEME: Jeremiah prophecies to remnant left in land

In these three chapters we find Jeremiah speaking to those who were left in the land of Judah after the destruction of Jerusalem. They were the very poor, the blind, the crippled, the lame, and another group which would be called the criminal element, a hard group of people. Jeremiah chose to stay with the people in the land. He had a message for them.

JEREMIAH RELEASED

The word that came to Jeremiah from the LORD, after that Nebuzaradan the captain of the guard had let him go from Ramah, when he had taken him being bound in chains among all that were carried away captive of Jerusalem and Judah, which were carried away captive unto Babylon.

And the captain of the guard took Jeremiah, and said unto him, The LORD thy God hath pronounced this evil upon this place.

Now the LORD hath brought it, and done according as he hath said: because ye have sinned against the LORD, and have not obeyed his voice, therefore this thing is come upon you.

And now, behold, I loose thee this day from the chains which were upon thine hand. If it seem good unto thee to come with me into Babylon, come; and I will look well unto thee: but if it seem ill unto thee to come with me into Babylon, forbear: behold, all the land is before thee: whither it seemeth good and convenient for thee to go, thither go [Jer. 40:1–4].

Nebuchadnezzar permitted Jeremiah to do what he wished to do. He could have gone with the captives to Babylon, but, interestingly enough, Jeremiah did not want to do that. I think he would have been given special privileges if he had gone, but Jeremiah couldn't bear to see his brethren suffer as they did there by the canals of Babylon where they sat down and hung up their harps and wept when they remembered Zion. Jeremiah did not want to go with them. They had rejected his message, and they had rejected him. In Babylon God would raise up another prophet, Ezekiel, who would speak to them. Jeremiah chose to remain in Judah with the poor remnant which were left there.

Who really loved that land? Jeremiah. Who was the real patriot? Jeremiah. Who really had the best interests of the people at heart? It was Jeremiah. This is quite obvious now.

You will remember that Jeremiah had urged them to surrender to Nebuchadnezzar. I believe that if they had obeyed God and gone willingly, they would not have gone into captivity. They probably would have received the kind of treatment that Jeremiah received from Nebuchadnezzar, and they probably would have been permitted to stay in the land.

Now in verse 8 we are introduced to Ishmael who plots to murder Gedaliah whom Nebuchadnezzar had made governor over the cities of Judah.

GEDALIAH MURDERED

In chapter 41 we have the bloody record of the slaying of Gedaliah with the Chaldeans and Jews who were with him. Then Ishmael captures the people of the city (Mizpah), intending to take them to the land of the Ammonites. They are overtaken by Johanan. Then Johanan, fearing the reprisal of the king of Babylon because his governor Gedaliah had been killed, plans to escape with the whole remnant of the people to Egypt.

JEREMIAH CONSULTED

In chapter 42 we see that before leaving for Egypt Johanan and all the captains come to Jeremiah. It is interesting that the people turned to Jeremiah under these strange circumstances. They needed to know what to do. Should they stay in the land or leave the land? Where should they go?

> **Then all the captains of the forces, and Johanan the son of Kareah, and Jezaniah the son of Hoshaiah, and all the people from the least even unto the greatest, came near,**
>
> **And said unto Jeremiah the prophet, Let, we beseech thee, our supplication be accepted before thee, and pray for us unto the LORD thy God, even for all this remnant; (for we are left but a few of many, as thine eyes do behold us:)**
>
> **That the LORD thy God may shew us the way wherein we may walk, and the thing that we may do [Jer. 42:1–3].**

This sounds very nice, doesn't it? You would think that these people would actually walk with God now. They promised to obey the voice of the Lord.

> **Then Jeremiah the prophet said unto them, I have heard you; behold, I will pray unto the LORD your God according to your words; and it shall come to pass, that whatsoever thing the LORD shall answer you, I will declare it unto you; I will keep nothing back from you [Jer. 42:4].**

They came to Jeremiah, and they knew that they could depend upon Jeremiah to speak the truth.

Any person who is attempting to speak for God, no matter whether his medium be the pulpit, radio, or even a soapbox, should lay aside all attempts at being clever and subtle. He should give forth the Word of God with no attempt at being sophisticated and saying smooth words to please the people. When the pulpit majors in positive thinking and ignores the negatives, it becomes weak and is only a sounding board just to say back to the people what they want to hear. Paul wrote to Timothy, "For the time will come when they will not endure sound doctrine; but after their own lusts shall they heap to themselves teachers, having itching ears; And they shall turn away their ears from the truth, and shall be turned unto fables" (2 Tim. 4:3–4). Unfortunately, I think that is much of what the modern pulpit is today. That is the reason it has become extremely weak and has no message for this hour in which we live. When the pulpit can give out God's Word as Jeremiah did, with nothing being held back, letting it say what God means for it to say, then the Word of God will become effective again in our day.

Now Jeremiah is going to tell the remnant exactly what God says they are to do—

> **And said unto them, Thus saith the LORD, the God of Israel, unto whom ye sent me to present your supplication before him;**
>
> **If ye will still abide in this land, then will I build you, and not pull you down, and I will plant you, and not pluck you up: for I repent me of the evil that I have done unto you [Jer. 42:9–10].**

God assures them that He will not continue to judge them if they will obey Him. After all, God wants to bless; judgment is His *strange* work.

> **Be not afraid of the king of Babylon, of whom ye are afraid; be not afraid of him, saith the LORD: for I am with you to save you, and to deliver you from his hand.**
>
> **And I will shew mercies unto you, that he may have mercy upon you, and cause you to return to your own land [Jer. 42:11–12].**

Jeremiah delivers the Word as the Lord gave it to him. It was a good word, an encouraging word. You would think by now they would know that Jeremiah spoke God's Word, because it had been proven true. You would think they would believe God, but God knows they won't. He adds this warning—

> For thus saith the LORD of hosts, the God of Israel; As mine anger and my fury hath been poured forth upon the inhabitants of Jerusalem; so shall my fury be poured forth upon you, when ye shall enter into Egypt: and ye shall be an execration, and an astonishment, and a curse, and a reproach; and ye shall see this place no more.

> The LORD hath said concerning you, O ye remnant of Judah; Go ye not into Egypt: know certainly that I have admonished you this day.

> For ye dissembled in your hearts, when ye sent me unto the LORD your God, saying, Pray for us unto the LORD our God; and according unto all that the LORD our God shall say, so declare unto us, and we will do it [Jer. 42:18–20].

Experience has taught them nothing. They still will not obey God. They will not hear the message from Jeremiah. God has told them not to go down into Egypt. So where will they go? They go to Egypt.

CHAPTERS 43 AND 44

THEME: Prophecies to remnant in Egypt

We have come now to the sixth and last section of prophecy of the Book of Jeremiah. This contains prophecies during Jeremiah's last days in Egypt and extends from chapters 43 to 51. Chapters 43 and 44 contain his words to the remnant in Egypt.

JEREMIAH'S MESSAGE REJECTED

And it came to pass, that when Jeremiah had made an end of speaking unto all the people all the words of the LORD their God, for which the LORD their God had sent him to them, even all these words,

Then spake Azariah the son of Hoshaiah, and Johanan the son of Kareah, and all the proud men, saying unto Jeremiah, Thou speakest falsely: the LORD our God hath not sent thee to say, Go not into Egypt to sojourn there:

But Baruch the son of Neriah setteth thee on against us, for to deliver us into the hand of the Chaldeans, that they might put us to death, and carry us away captives into Babylon [Jer. 43:1–3].

These people go through the same routine again. They say that God hadn't really told Jeremiah to say that. The problem is that he is not saying what they want him to say. They had hoped he would tell them to go to Egypt. Instead, God tells them not to go into Egypt.

But Johanan the son of Kareah, and all the captains of the forces, took all the remnant of Judah, that were returned from all nations, whither they had been driven, to dwell in the land of Judah;

Even men, and women, and children, and the king's daughters, and every person that Nebuzaradan the captain of the guard had left with Gedaliah the son of Ahikam the son of Shaphan, and Jeremiah the prophet, and Baruch the son of Neriah.

So they came into the land of Egypt: for they obeyed not the voice of the LORD: thus came they even to Tahpanhes [Jer. 43:5–7].

Johanan and the captains forced the remnant into Egypt, including the prophet Jeremiah. So they return to Tahpanhes, a place near where they had begun as a nation in the land of Goshen in Egypt. They forced Jeremiah to go with them against his will, but he still is speaking to them.

JEREMIAH'S WARNING TO THE
REMNANT IN EGYPT

Then came the word of the LORD unto Jeremiah in Tahpanhes, saying,

Take great stones in thine hand, and hide them in the clay in the brickkiln, which is at the entry of Pharaoh's house in Tahpanhes, in the sight of the men of Judah [Jer. 43:8–9].

They are back down in the brickyards of Egypt. We can see that disobedience to God does not help them to advance—they are right back where they started.

And say unto them, Thus saith the LORD of hosts, the God of Israel; Behold, I will send and take Nebuchadrezzar, the king of Babylon, my servant, and will set his throne upon these stones that I have hid; and he shall spread his royal pavilion over them.

> **And when he cometh, he shall smite the land of Egypt, and deliver such as are for death to death; and such as are for captivity to captivity; and such as are for the sword to the sword [Jer. 43:10–11].**

They ran off to the land of Egypt to escape from Nebuchadnezzar, but God is going to permit Nebuchadnezzar to take the land of Egypt. They are worse off than if they had obeyed God and stayed in the land. They will be right back under Nebuchadnezzar; but now they are out of the land, and Nebuchadnezzar will put them into slavery.

THE REMNANT IN EGYPT REJECTS GOD

Chapter 44 records the absolute refusal of the remnant in Egypt to obey God.

Again God patiently explains that He is the One responsible for the invasion and desolation of Judah.

> **Thus saith the LORD of hosts, the God of Israel; Ye have seen all the evil that I have brought upon Jerusalem, and upon all the cities of Judah; and, behold, this day they are a desolation, and no man dwelleth therein,**

> **Because of their wickedness which they have committed to provoke me to anger, in that they went to burn incense, and to serve other gods, whom they knew not, neither they, ye, nor your fathers [Jer. 44:2–3].**

Again God gives the reason for His punishment.

> **Therefore now thus saith the LORD, the God of hosts, the God of israel; Wherefore commit ye this great evil against your souls, to cut off from you man and woman, child and suckling, out of Judah, to leave you none to remain;**

> In that ye provoke me unto wrath with the works of your hands, burning incense unto other gods in the land of Egypt, whither ye be gone to dwell, that ye might cut yourselves off, and that ye might be a curse and a reproach among all the nations of the earth? [Jer. 44:7–8].

What a revelation of God's love! He still pleads with them to return to Him.

Their insolent reply is an example of the utter depravity of the human heart.

> As for the word that thou hast spoken unto us in the name of the LORD, we will not hearken unto thee.
>
> But we will certainly do whatsoever thing goeth forth out of our own mouth, to burn incense unto the queen of heaven, and to pour out drink offerings unto her, as we have done, we, and our fathers, our kings, and our princes, in the cities of Judah, and in the streets of Jerusalem: for then had we plenty of victuals, and were well, and saw no evil [Jer. 44:16–17].

There is nothing left for them now but judgment.

CHAPTER 45

THEME: Prophecy to Baruch

Baruch was a friend who acted as sort of an assistant to Jeremiah. He was the one who wrote the words of Jeremiah on the scroll which was sent to King Jehoiakim, and the king cut the scroll with a knife and pitched it into the fire (ch. 36). When Jeremiah was in prison and bought the property in Anathoth, Baruch carried out the transaction for him. He had the papers signed and carried through with all the necessary work for the purchase of the land (ch. 32). Finally, Baruch was taken down into Egypt with Jeremiah according to chapter 43:6.

The prophecy to Baruch which we have here in chapter 45 was actually given during the reign of Jehoiakim. That is the reason we said at the beginning of the book that although there is a certain semblance of chronological order in the Book of Jeremiah, it is not arranged chronologically. Although the prophecy was given back during the reign of Jehoiakim, it is recorded here, and I think there is a reason for that. I believe it is recorded here as an encouragement to Baruch. The Lord had already revealed to him what would happen to him if he identified himself with Jeremiah the prophet. This should be an encouragement to him when he was forced to go to Egypt with the remnant of Judah.

> **Thus saith the LORD, the God of Israel, unto thee, O Baruch;**
>
> **Thou didst say, Woe is me now! for the LORD hath added grief to my sorrow; I fainted in my sighing, and I find no rest [Jer. 45:2–3].**

Things were pretty bad during the reign of Jehoiakim, but that was nothing compared with what was going to follow. The really bad time would occur after the era of Jehoiakim.

> Thus shalt thou say unto him, The LORD saith thus: Behold, that which I have built will I break down, and that which I have planted I will pluck up, even this whole land [Jer. 45:4].

Even though things were going to get very much worse, God wanted Baruch to know that He was the One who was responsible for it. God assumed responsibility for what would happen to the land of Judah; therefore, Baruch could go along with the program.

> And seekest thou great things for thyself? seek them not: for, behold, I will bring evil upon all flesh, saith the LORD: but thy life will I give unto thee for a prey in all places whither thou goest [Jer. 45:5].

This prophecy was given to Baruch when he was still a young man. God told him that he couldn't expect to arrive at some high goal for himself at this tragic time in the history of the nation. He would live through very troubled times, but he would come through it with his life because God would preserve him. Now Jeremiah and Baruch, his friend and associate, are old men in Egypt. They have seen how God did preserve them through the troubled times in which they lived.

CHAPTERS 46—48

THEME: Prophecy to Egypt, Philistia, and Moab

Jeremiah is in Egypt, having been taken there against his will by the remnant who disobeyed God and went to Egypt. Now Jeremiah gives prophecies to the different nations round about.

God tells them what will happen to Egypt. The remnant which left from Judah went down to Egypt because they thought they would have peace and plenty there. God says, "I have news for you: the war is going to move down to Egypt, and Nebuchadnezzar will take Egypt, too"—which he did.

> **They did cry there, Pharaoh king of Egypt is but a noise;**
> **he hath passed the time appointed [Jer. 46:17].**

In other words, they can't depend on Pharaoh any longer. Egypt will go down in defeat.

> **O thou daughter dwelling in Egypt, furnish thyself to go**
> **into captivity: for Noph shall be waste and desolate**
> **without an inhabitant [Jer. 46:19].**

The survivors of Judah made a big mistake to put their trust in Pharaoh and in Egypt. They should have put their trust in God. They should have believed and obeyed the Lord. Yet, in spite of all that, Jeremiah includes a wonderful prophecy of comfort to them.

> **But fear not thou, O my servant Jacob, and be not dis-**
> **mayed, O Israel: for, behold, I will save thee from afar**
> **off, and thy seed from the land of their captivity; and**
> **Jacob shall return, and be in rest and at ease, and none**
> **shall make him afraid.**

> **Fear thou not, O Jacob my servant, saith the LORD: for I
> am with thee; for I will make a full end of all the nations
> whither I have driven thee: but I will not make a full end
> of thee, but correct thee in measure; yet will I not leave
> thee wholly unpunished [Jer. 46:27–28].**

My friend, after you read these two verses, if you believe the Word of God to be true, you must believe that God is not through with the nation of Israel. God tells them He must punish them but that He will not make a full end of them. Here is one of the many answers to the question ". . . Hath God cast away his people? . . ." (Rom. 11:1). If we believe the Word of God, we must let this Word stand and accept it at face value.

Chapter 47 gives the prophecy of Jeremiah against the Philistine country.

This little remnant from Judah began to look from one nation to another. Where should they go? On which nation might they depend? Some of these nations were their enemies. Should they go to them for refuge? The answer is no because the land of the Philistines will be conquered also.

In chapter 48 we see a prophecy against Moab. Moab ceases from being a nation.

> **And Moab shall be destroyed from being a people, be-
> cause he hath magnified himself against the LORD [Jer.
> 48:42].**

The present-day Hashemite Kingdom of Jordan on the east bank of the Jordan River occupies the same land that the country of Moab and the people of Moab once occupied. Yet God is not through with the people of Moab. I don't know where they are today; I doubt whether anyone could locate them. But God is able to locate them—

> **Yet will I bring again the captivity of Moab in the latter
> days, saith the LORD. Thus far is the judgment of Moab
> [Jer. 48:47].**

God will bring again the captivity of Moab in the latter days. Evidently Moab will enter the Millennium. However, at the time of Jeremiah, there was no use for the people to flee to Moab. They wouldn't be safe there either.

CHAPTER 49

THEME: *Prophecies to nations surrounding Israel*

We have seen that the people who had been left in Judah made the mistake of going down into Egypt. They went there in disobedience to God, and they went out of the frying pan into the fire. The war was over in the land of Israel. No enemy would want to come in to take that land now. The cities had been absolutely run over, burned, left with nothing but debris. Only the ashes of a former civilization were left there. The remnant should have stayed. They could have built up their land, but instead they ran off to Egypt. God knew that Egypt would be the area of the next big campaign of Nebuchadnezzar. When he took Egypt, he would take these people for the second time. They would be captured again and would suffer again. They thought they were running away from war. They thought they were going to a land where they would have plenty to eat. They thought only of safety and full stomachs.

My friend, when our attitudes and actions and goals are not based on a desire to live for God, when God's truth is no longer our guide, we have sunk to a low level which won't bring peace or plenty. This has been the experience down through the annals of history. History has great lessons to teach us if we will but listen.

This chapter continues God's prophecies through Jeremiah concerning the judgment which was coming to the nations surrounding Israel.

PROPHECY TO AMMON

The remnant of Judah need not look to Ammon for shelter, because it will be destroyed. There is no nation of Ammon in our day, but notice what God says—

> **And afterward I will bring again the captivity of the children of Ammon, saith the LORD [Jer. 49:6].**

Ammon is to be restored.

These are remarkable prophecies, remarkable verses of Scripture.

PROPHECY TO EDOM

There is more space given to the prophecy directed to Edom—probably because Edom was related to Israel. Esau and Jacob were brothers, and the two nations Edom and Israel have not come from these two men. Edom and Israel have not been friendly down through the years. Edom had become a great nation, for God had said that He would make a great nation out of Esau.

> **Concerning Edom, thus saith the Lord of hosts; Is wisdom no more in Teman? is counsel perished from the prudent? is their wisdom vanished?**

> **Flee ye, turn back, dwell deep, O inhabitants of Dedan; for I will bring the calamity of Esau upon him, the time that I will visit him [Jer. 49:7–8].**

Edom was in the territory that is south and more to the east of the Dead Sea, an area between the Dead Sea and the Gulf of 'Aqaba. Edom was in for a judgment from God. They had become a great nation and had furnished advisors to other nations. The rock-hewn city of Petra was such a secure place that it acted as a depository for the great nations. Both Babylon and Egypt carries a bank account there. This was a place where they could store their treasures and feel safe about them. The city was hewn out of solid rock on both sides, and there was only one little entrance into this rock-hewn city. It was a tremendous place in its day, but God took away all the greatness which it once enjoyed. Their greatness depended largely on the nations round about them that looked to them because they felt Petra was so secure.

> **For I have sworn by myself, saith the Lord, that Bozrah shall become a desolation, a reproach, a waste, and a curse; and all the cities thereof shall be perpetual wastes [Jer. 49:13].**

Bozrah is Petra and Edom. That rock-hewn city is still there today, completely deserted. It is a ready-made city, and if you are looking for an apartment, I can tell you where you can get one that is rent free. Those rock-hewn apartments are lovely, and you could move into one tomorrow if you wished to do so. It's all there today, and you can have it. No one will come around to collect the rent. No one will try to sell you any of the property. I caution you, however, that you won't stay there very long. People who have tried to live there just don't stay. Some years ago the Germans tried to colonize Petra. The colony that was sent into Petra didn't make a go of it, and before long the people scattered.

> **Thy terribleness hath deceived thee, and the pride of thine heart, O thou that dwellest in the clefts of the rock, that holdest the height of the hill: though thou shouldest make thy nest as high as the eagle, I will bring thee down from thence, saith the LORD [Jer. 49:16].**

The great sin of the Edomites was pride, and for this they were judged. They were in a place that was remarkably protected. The entrance to Petra was through a deep and narrow defile, called the Sik, which was about a mile in length. It was just sort of a cleft in the rock in the valley known as the Wadi Musa. The nation had a history of about one thousand years. Then the Nabataean Arabs took it. The Greeks made two fruitless expeditions against it but found it to be an impregnable city. It was inaccessible for modern men until the airplane. We have had the experience of going into the city of Petra with some of our tours and have found it a remarkable place.

The city was influenced by Babylon, Egypt, Greece, and Rome. One can see it in the architecture and the remnants of their civilization. God judged Edom and brought her down.

Now God says this concerning it, and Ezekiel has a more complete prophecy—

> **Also Edom shall be a desolation: every one that goeth by it shall be astonished, and shall hiss at all the plagues thereof.**

As in the overthrow of Sodom and Gomorrah and the neighbour cities thereof, saith the LORD, no man shall abide there, neither shall a son of man dwell in it [Jer. 49:17–18].

This is a prophecy which has been literally fulfilled. The city is still there. It cannot be destroyed since it is hewn right into the rocks. God said it would not be inhabited, and it isn't. Every now and then an Arab pitches his tent there for the night, but he's on his way the next day. The Arabs have very superstitious feelings about the city. Although the Germans didn't have superstitious feelings, they couldn't colonize it either. The Word of God says that "neither shall a son of man dwell in it." It is a ready-made city; yet it will not become an abiding place for men.

This is even more remarkable when you place this prophecy beside the prophecy against Tyre. God had said that Tyre would be scraped so that there would be absolutely nothing left of it, but that it would be inhabited after that. Tyre is an inhabited city today. In contrast, Petra is a city that has never been destroyed yet is without an inhabitant.

Therefore hear the counsel of the LORD, that he hath taken against Edom; and his purposes, that he hath purposed against the inhabitants of Teman: Surely the least of the flock shall draw them out: surely he shall make their habitations desolate with them [Jer. 49:20].

The city has become desolate, and the nation of Edom has disappeared.

PROPHECY TO DAMASCUS

Concerning Damascus. Hamath is confounded, and Arpad: for they have heard evil tidings: they are fainthearted; there is sorrow on the sea; it cannot be quiet.

Damascus is waxed feeble, and turneth herself to flee, and fear hath seized on her: anguish and sorrows have taken her, as a woman in travail [Jer. 49:23–24].

Damascus is said to be the oldest inhabited city. There are many other cities that make the same claim, but Damascus probably has some right to it. Here is a prophecy against Damascus stating that the city would be destroyed. It has been destroyed, and it has shifted its position several times. However, the name Damascus continues on with the city, and today it is the capital of Syria.

PROPHECY TO KEDAR, HAZOR, ELAM

Then there is a prophecy against two very prosperous places, Kedar and Hazor. We know very little about them. They were told that Nebuchadnezzar would smite them, and he did. Then there is also a prophecy against Elam.

Thus saith the Lord of hosts; Behold, I will break the bow of Elam, the chief of their might [Jer. 49:35].

Elam is to be destroyed but will be restored in "the latter days" (v. 39).

All of these nations are to suffer the same fate as Israel, so that there is no place for the remnant of Judah to flee for safety. They could turn to no one for help. They looked every place but up. Their only help was in the Lord, but they did not turn to Him. He had given them direction, but they would not receive it.

They, of course, decided to go to Egypt—to their ultimate destruction.

CHAPTERS 50 AND 51

THEME: Prophecy to Babylon

Here is the prophecy against the nation which at that time was the top nation of the world. It was the first great world power but would also be destroyed. Judgment would come to Babylon.

> **The word that the LORD spake against Babylon and against the land of the Chaldeans by Jeremiah the prophet.**
>
> **Declare ye among the nations, and publish, and set up a standard; publish, and conceal not: say, Babylon is taken, Bel is confounded, Merodach is broken in pieces; her idols are confounded, her images are broken in pieces [Jer. 50:1–2].**

When this was written, it looked as if Israel would disappear from the face of the earth and that Babylon would continue as a world power. Yet God says that Babylon would be destroyed.

> **In those days, and in that time, saith the LORD, the children of Israel shall come, they and the children of Judah together, going and weeping: they shall go, and seek the LORD their God [Jer. 50:4].**

Israel will survive. This prophecy looks forward to the last days when Israel will turn to God.

God says he will judge Babylon; she shall be conquered by the Medo-Persians—

> **For, lo, I will raise and cause to come up against Babylon an assembly of great nations from the north country: and they shall set themselves in array against her;**

> **from thence she shall be taken: their arrows shall be as
> of a mighty expert man; none shall return in vain [Jer.
> 50:9].**

It was by a clever maneuver that Gobryas was able to invade Babylon.

> **Because of the wrath of the LORD it shall not be inhab-
> ited, but it shall be wholly desolate: every one that goeth
> by Babylon shall be astonished, and hiss at all her
> plagues [Jer. 50:13].**

That this verse has been literally fulfilled is obvious to every tourist
who visits the ruins of ancient Babylon.

> **Israel is a scattered sheep; the lions have driven him
> away: first the king of Assyria hath devoured him; and
> last this Nebuchadrezzar king of Babylon hath broken
> his bones.**

> **Therefore thus saith the LORD of hosts, the God of Israel;
> Behold, I will punish the king of Babylon and his land,
> as I have punished the king of Assyria [Jer. 50:17–18].**

The destruction of Babylon will come suddenly and take her unaware.

> **I have laid a snare for thee, and thou art also taken, O
> Babylon, and thou wast not aware: thou art found, and
> also caught, because thou hast striven against the LORD
> [Jer. 50:24].**

You can read the account of this in Daniel 5.

> **Come against her from the utmost border, open her
> storehouses: cast her up as heaps, and destroy her ut-
> terly: let nothing of her be left [Jer. 50:26].**

You can look at Babylon today; it is a heap of ruins. It was utterly
destroyed.

> The voice of them that flee and escape out of the land of
> Babylon, to declare in Zion the vengeance of the LORD
> our God, the vengeance of his temple [Jer. 50:28].

The report of the destruction of Babylon is to be announced in Zion.

> A drought is upon her waters; and they shall be dried
> up: for it is the land of graven images, and they are mad
> upon their idols.
>
> Therefore the wild beasts of the desert with the wild
> beasts of the islands shall dwell there, and the owls
> shall dwell therein: and it shall be no more inhabited for
> ever; neither shall it be dwelt in from generation to gen-
> eration.
>
> As God overthrew Sodom and Gomorrah and the neigh-
> bour cities thereof, saith the LORD; so shall no man abide
> there, neither shall any son of man dwell therein [Jer.
> 50:38–40].

The destruction of Babylon is compared to the destruction of Sodom
and Gomorrah.

> They shall hold the bow and the lance: they are cruel,
> and will not shew mercy: their voice shall roar like the
> sea, and they shall ride upon horses, every one put in
> array, like a man to the battle, against thee, O daughter
> of Babylon [Jer. 50:42].

This is exactly what happened when Gobryas, the Median, entered
the city.

Chapter 51 continues the prediction of God's judgment on Babylon.

> Flee out of the midst of Babylon, and deliver every man
> his soul: be not cut off in her iniquity; for this is the time
> of the LORD'S vengeance; he will render unto her a rec-
> ompence.

> Babylon hath been a golden cup in the LORD'S hand, that made all the earth drunken: the nations have drunken of her wine; therefore the nations are mad.
>
> Babylon is suddenly fallen and destroyed: howl for her; take balm for her pain, if so be she may be healed [Jer. 51:6–8].

Babylon was to be destroyed suddenly—that, of course, was literally fulfilled.

> Behold, I am against thee, O destroying mountain, saith the LORD, which destroyest all the earth: and I will stretch out mine hand upon thee, and roll thee down from the rocks, and will make thee a burnt mountain.
>
> And they shall not take of thee a stone for a corner, nor a stone for foundations; but thou shalt be desolate for ever, saith the LORD [Jer. 51:25–26].

And it certainly is desolate today.

> Therefore thus saith the LORD; Behold, I will plead thy cause, and take vengeance for thee; and I will dry up her sea, and make her springs dry.
>
> And Babylon shall become heaps, a dwellingplace for dragons, an astonishment, and an hissing, without an inhabitant [Jer. 51:36–37].

Note that this utter desolation is to follow, not some future overthrow, but the sack of the city resulting from the turning aside of the waters of the river. The Euphrates River, which flowed directly through Babylon, was diverted from its course, which left an entryway at each end for the warriors of the enemy to enter under the walls in the dry riverbed. By this maneuver they were able to appear suddenly in the streets and take the city by surprise.

CHAPTER 52

THEME: Fulfillment of the prophesied destruction of Jerusalem

We have already briefly looked at this chapter because it is a review in retrospect of the destruction of Jerusalem and the captivity of Judah. What Jeremiah had first given as prophecy he now writes as history. He recounts again the capture of King Zedekiah and tells how his sons were slain and his eyes put out by the king of Babylon.

Jeremiah also tells us what happened to Jehoiachin after he had been captured and taken to Babylon:

> And it came to pass in the seven and thirtieth year of the captivity of Jehoiachin king of Judah, in the twelfth month, in the five and twentieth day of the month, that Evil-merodach king of Babylon in the first year of his reign lifted up the head of Jehoiachin king of Judah, and brought him forth out of prison.
>
> And spake kindly unto him, and set his throne above the throne of the kings that were with him in Babylon.
>
> And changed his prison garments: and he did continually eat bread before him all the days of his life.
>
> And for his diet, there was a continual diet given him of the king of Babylon, every day a portion until the day of his death, all the days of his life [Jer. 52:31–34].

Jehoiachin died in Babylon. Jeremiah had prophesied that no king from this line would again sit on the throne of David; this ends the line of David through his son Solomon. The Son of David who will sit on that throne through all eternity was born through another line, the line of Nathan. Mary was born in that line, and it is in that line that Jesus Christ has claim to the throne of David. This is why the Book of Jeremiah ends with these important details about the royal line.

BIBLIOGRAPHY

(Recommended for Further Study)

Feinberg, Charles L. *Jeremiah*. Grand Rapids, Michigan: Zondervan Publishing House, 1982. (Excellent, comprehensive treatment.)

Gaebelein, Arno C. *The Annotated Bible*. Neptune, New Jersey: Loizeaux Brothers, 1917.

Gray, James M. *Synthetic Bible Studies*. Old Tappan, New Jersey: Fleming H. Revell Co., 1906.

Ironside, H. A. *Notes on Jeremiah*. Neptune, New Jersey: Loizeaux Brothers, 1946.

Jensen, Irving L. *Jeremiah: Prophet of Judgment*. Chicago, Illinois: Moody Press, 1966.

Jensen, Irving L. *Isaiah and Jeremiah*. Chicago, Illinois: Moody Press. (A self-study guide.)

Meyer, F. B. *Jeremiah: Priest and Prophet*. Fort Washington, Pennsylvania: Christian Literature Crusade, 1894. (A rich devotional study.)

Sauer, Erich. *The Dawn of World Redemption*. Grand Rapids, Michigan: Wm. B. Eerdmans Publishing Co., 1951. (An excellent Old Testament survey.)

Scroggie, W. Graham. *The Unfolding Drama of Redemption*. Grand Rapids, Michigan: Zondervan Publishing House, 1970. (An excellent survey and outline of the Old Testament.)

Unger, Merrill F. *Unger's Commentary on the Old Testament*. Chicago, Illinois: Moody Press, 1982. (Highly recommended.)

HELPFUL BOOKS ON BIBLE PROPHECY

Hoyt, Hermann A. *The End Times*. Chicago, Illinois: Moody Press, 1969.

Pentecost, J. Dwight. *Things to Come*. Grand Rapids, Michigan: Zondervan Publishing House, 1958.

Ryrie, Charles C. *The Basis of the Premillennial Faith*. Neptune, New Jersey: Loizeaux Brothers, 1953.

Ryrie, Charles C. *What You Should Know About the Rapture*. Chicago, Illinois: Moody Press, 1981.

Sauer, Erich. *From Eternity to Eternity*. Grand Rapids, Michigan: Wm. B. Eerdmans Publishing Co., 1954.

Unger, Merrill F. *Beyond the Crystal Ball*. Chicago, Illinois: Moody Press, 1973.

Walvoord, John F. *Armageddon, Oil, and the Middle East Crisis*. Grand Rapids, Michigan: Zondervan Publishing House, 1974.

Walvoord, John F. *The Millennial Kingdom*. Grand Rapids, Michigan: Zondervan Publishing House, 1959.

Walvoord, John F. *The Rapture Question*. Grand Rapids, Michigan: Zondervan Publishing House, 1957.

Wood, Leon J. *The Bible and Future Events*. Grand Rapids, Michigan: Zondervan Publishing House, 1973.

LAMENTATIONS

The Book of
LAMENTATIONS

INTRODUCTION

The Book of Lamentations normally and naturally follows the prophecy of Jeremiah. In this little book the soul of the prophet is laid bare before us. These are the lamentations of Jeremiah.

Dr. Alexander Whyte, one of the great expositors of the Word of God of days gone by, has said: "There is nothing like the Lamentations of Jeremiah in the whole world. There has been plenty of sorrow in every age, and in every land, but such another preacher and author, with such a heart for sorrow, has never again been born. Dante comes next to Jeremiah, and we know that Jeremiah was the great exile's favorite prophet."

Jeremiah began his ministry during the reign of Josiah. Both he and Josiah were young men, and they were evidently friends. It was Josiah who led the last revival in Judah. It was a revival in which a great many hearts were touched, but on the whole it proved to be largely a surface movement. Josiah met his untimely death in the battle at Megiddo against Pharaoh-nechoh, a battle that Josiah never should have been in. Jeremiah, however, continued his prophetic ministry during the reigns of the four wretched kings who followed Josiah: Jehoahaz, Jeoiakim, Jehoiachin, and Zedekiah, the last king of Judah. His was a harsh message as he attempted to call his people and his nation back to God, but he was never able to deter the downward course of Judah. He witnessed the destruction of Jerusalem; and as he saw it burn, he sat down in the warm ashes, hot tears coursing down his cheeks.

The Book of Lamentations is composed of five chapters, and each chapter is an elegy, almost a funeral dirge. These elegies are sad beyond description. In them we see Jeremiah as he stood over Jerusalem weeping. This book is filled with tears and sorrow. It is a paean of pain, a poem of pity, a proverb of pathos. It is a hymn of heartbreak, a psalm of sadness, a symphony of sorrow, and a story of sifting. Lamentations is the wailing wall of the Bible.

Lamentations moves us into the very heart of Jeremiah. He gave a message from God that actually broke his heart. How tragic and wretched he was. If you were to pour his tears into a test tube to analyze them from a scientific viewpoint and determine how much sodium chloride, or salt, they contained, you still would not know the sorrow and the heartbreak of this man. He has been called the prophet of the broken heart. His was a life filled with pathos and pity. His sobbing was a solo. Ella Wheeler Wilcox has written a piece of doggerel that goes like this:

> Laugh, and the world laughs with you;
> Weep, and you weep alone:
> For this sad old earth must borrow its mirth,
> But it has trouble enough of its own.

Tears are generally conceded to be a sign of weakness, crying is effeminate, and bawling is for babies. Years ago when I was pastor of a church here in Pasadena where I still live, the playground for our summer Bible school was right outside my study window. One little boy brought his even younger sister, and it was interesting to watch how he hovered over her and watched after her. Neither one of them was very big. But one day she fell on the asphalt and scratched her knee. She began to cry, as a little child would. He tried to give her a sales talk in order to quiet her down. Oh, she shouldn't cry, he said, only women cry. Well, I don't know what he thought she was, but nevertheless it worked, and she stopped crying.

This man Jeremiah had a woman's heart. He was sensitive. He was sincere. He was sympathetic. He was as tender as a mother. Yet he gave the strongest and harshest message in the Bible: he announced the destruction of Jerusalem, and he pronounced judgment, counseling the people to surrender to Nebuchadnezzar. His message did nothing but get him into all kinds of trouble.

Now what kind of a man would you have chosen to deliver such a rough, brutal, tough message as that? Would you have wanted Attila the Hun or a Hitler or a Mussolini? Of one thing I am sure: none of us would send Casper Milquetoast to give the message! But God did choose such a man, a man with a tender heart.

Dr. G. Campbell Morgan tells the story about Dr. Dale of Birmingham who used to say that Dwight L. Moody was the only man who seemed to him to have the right to preach about hell. When someone asked Dr. Dale why he said that, he replied, "Because he always preaches it with tears in his voice." That is the type of man God wants today. We have too many who are not moved by the message they give.

David Garrick, one of the great Shakespearean actors of the past, told about the day he was walking down the street in London and found a man standing on the corner just yearning over the people. Garrick said, "I stood on the outside of the crowd, but I found myself imperceptibly working my way in, until I stood right under that man, and there came down from his breast hot tears." He went on to say that there was a woman there, pointing her shaking, withered finger at the man who spoke, and she said, "Sir, I have followed you since you preached this morning at seven o'clock and I have heard you preach five times in the streets of this city, and five times I have been wet with your tears. Why do you weep?" That preacher was George Whitefield, a cross-eyed man who was burlesqued on the English stage and denounced from almost every pulpit in the country. David Garrick went on to say, "I listened to George Whitefield, and as I listened to him I saw his passion and his earnestness. I knew that he meant that without Christ men would die. As I listened to him, he came to the place where he could say nothing more. He reached up those mighty arms, his voice seemed almost like a thunderstorm as he said one final word: 'Oh!'" Why, he could break an audience with that word! When George Whitefield said "Oh!" men bowed before the Holy Spirit like corn bows under the wind. Garrick went on, "I would give my hand full of golden sovereigns if I could say 'Oh!' like George Whitefield. I would be the greatest actor that the world has ever known." The only difference was that George Whitefield was sincere—he was not acting. Jeremiah was that kind of a preacher also.

I am afraid that we have developed a generation in our day that has no feeling, no compassion for this lost world. There is little concern for getting out the Word of God. There is little attention given to moral fiber or a high sense of duty.

Several years ago in a *Reader's Digest* article, young people were counseled that their highest chances of success in life would be found "by engaging in work you most enjoy doing, and which gives fullest expression to your abilities and personality." If Jeremiah had read that article and heeded its advice, he probably would have gone into some other kind of business. But Jeremiah could say that it was the Word of God that he rejoiced in: "Thy words were found, and I did eat them; and thy word was unto me the joy and rejoicing of mine heart: for I am called by thy name, O LORD God of hosts" (Jer. 15:16). How wonderful this man was!

The young people today who have been trained—even many in Christian work—are simply looking for a job where they can punch a clock, go home to watch TV, and forget all about it. They hold their feelings and emotions in reserve and are unwilling to become really involved in getting out the Word of God.

I don't always understand Jeremiah, but I admire him and look up to him. Mrs. Elizabeth Cook wrote this about him:

> A woman's heart—tender and quick and warm;
> But man's in iron will and courage strong.
> His harp was set to weird, pathetic song,
> Yet when time called for deeds, no wrathful storm
> From throne or altar could his soul disarm—
> His disheartening battle fierce and long.

This is Jeremiah, the man who had a sorrow.

Jeremiah reminds us of Another who sat weeping over Jerusalem. The only difference is that Jerusalem was in ruins and the temple already burned as Jeremiah gazed upon the debris. Jesus wept over the same city about six centuries later because of what was going to happen to her. To Jeremiah the destruction of Jerusalem was a matter of history. To Jesus the destruction of Jerusalem was a matter of prophecy.

The key verse in the Book of Lamentations explains the reason Jerusalem lay in ruin: "The LORD is righteous; for I have rebelled against his commandment: hear, I pray you, all people, and behold my sorrow: my virgins and my young men are gone into captivity" (Lam. 1:18).

CHAPTER 1

THEME: Elegy 1

The first elegy in Lamentations opens on a doleful note. Jeremiah is singing in a minor key.

> **How doth the city sit solitary, that was full of people! how is she become as a widow! she that was great among the nations, and princess among the provinces, how is she become tributary! [Lam. 1:1].**

The great city of Jerusalem has fallen. What is the explanation? Jeremiah makes two tremendous statements that will help us understand.

> **Jerusalem hath grievously sinned; therefore she is removed: all that honoured her despise her, because they have seen her nakedness: yea, she sigheth, and turneth backward [Lam. 1:8].**

"Jerusalem hath grievously sinned"—this is the first explanation for the fall of the city. Her nakedness was revealed—what a picture!

> **Is it nothing to you, all ye that pass by? behold, and see if there be any sorrow like unto my sorrow, which is done unto me, wherewith the LORD hath afflicted me in the day of his fierce anger [Lam. 1:12].**

People don't like to hear about the fierce anger of God today. That aspect is often left out of the gospel message, and I have observed this particularly in the religious programs that are shown on TV, even by so-called gospel churches. In one Christmas program I saw, they did say that Christ was born of a virgin and that He was God manifest in the flesh—I rejoiced in that. But the program was a travesty of the gospel because it said that Christ came to give you a new personality, to bring peace and love—and oh, how insipid it was! It was a message for comfort and for compromise. The excuse that is often given for such an approach with the gospel is that it is trying to reach the man of the world. Jeremiah, too, was trying to reach a lost world, and he wasn't very successful; but at least he gave God's message as God had given it to him. God judged Judah because of her sin, and He still will judge sin today.

> **The LORD is righteous; for I have rebelled against his commandment: hear, I pray you, all people, and behold my sorrow: my virgins and my young men are gone into captivity [Lam. 1:18].**

Jeremiah mourned the destruction of Jerusalem alone. He stood among the ashes weeping. Why had the city been destroyed? The city had sinned. The second explanation is "The LORD is righteous." God did it, and God was right in what He did.

This is difficult to understand, and I must say I feel totally inadequate to deal with this. I merely stand at the fringe of the sorrow of this man and find I cannot enter in. I can merely look over the wall into his garden; I am not able to walk up and down in it. He has revealed two things to us, the bitter and the sweet: Jerusalem has sinned, yet God loves Jerusalem. "Jerusalem hath grievously sinned," and "the LORD is righteous." God loved them, He said, "with an everlasting love." He brought this upon them because He is righteous.

A statement from G. Campbell Morgan may help us to understand this. Of the revelation of God's anger, he said: "This is a supreme necessity in the interest of the universe. Prisons are in the interest of the free. Hell is the safeguard of heaven. A state that cannot punish crime is doomed; and a God Who tolerates evil is not good. Deny me my Biblical revelation of the anger of God, and I am insecure in the universe. But reveal to me this Throne established, occupied by One Whose heart is full of tenderness, Whose bowels yearn with love; then I am assured that He will not tolerate that which blights and blasts and damns; but will destroy it, and all its instruments, in the interest of that which is high and noble and pure" (*Studies in the Prophecy of Jeremiah*, p. 248).

You and I are living in a universe where there is a God, a living God, a God whose heart goes out in love and yearning over you. But I want to say this to you: if you turn your back on Him, He will judge you even though He still loves you. He is the righteous God of this universe. I am not sure I understand all that, but I know it is what He says in His Word. Someday He will make it clear to us that hell is actually there because He is a God of love and a God of righteousness and a God of holiness. The whole universe, including Satan himself, will admit that God is righteous and just in all He does. My friend, God is so great and wonderful and good we dare not trifle with Him.

Jesus could say to the scribes and Pharisees, the religious leaders of His day, "Woe unto you, scribes and Pharisees, hypocrites!" Why did He call them hypocrites? Because ". . . ye devour widows' houses . . ." (Matt. 23:14)—that was one of the reasons. My friend, if your Christianity does not affect your heart, your life in your home and in your business, and your social life, then you are a hypocrite. I didn't say it; He said it, my beloved. And He is the One who wept over these men. My eyes are dry, but His eyes are filled with tears for you and for me today. Oh, my friend, don't turn your back on the God who loves you like this! It will be tragic indeed if you do.

God does what He does because He is a righteous God. He cannot shut his eyes to evil. When His own children disobey Him, God must discipline them, even though it breaks His heart. Jeremiah reveals to us the heart of God: when Jeremiah weeps, God is weeping; when he sorrows, God is sorrowing. When we don't understand what is happening, the important thing is to trust in knowing that God is righteous in what He does. Although it broke His heart, He was right in letting Jerusalem be destroyed and in letting the people go into captivity.

G. Smith wrote a poem about Jerusalem that gives us some insight into this man Jeremiah:

> I am the man sore smitten with the wrath
>   Of Him who fashion'd me; my heart is faint,

And crieth out, "Spare, spare, O God! Thy
    saint";
But yet with darkness doth He hedge my path.

My eyes with streams of fiery tears run down
    To see the daughter of my people slain,
    And in Jerusalem the godless reign;
Trouble on trouble are upon me thrown.

Mine adversaries clap their sinful hands
    The while they hiss and wag their heads, and
        say,
    "Where is the temple but of yesterday—
The noblest city of a hundred lands?"
We do confess our guilt; then, Lord, arise,
Avenge, avenge us of our enemies!

Jeremiah cries out—he wants to know why, and God assures him that He is righteous, right, in what He is doing to Jerusalem.

Another anguished question that Jeremiah has is this: "Is it nothing to you, all ye that pass by?" (v. 12). In other words, How much are the people involved? Do they really care?

Man does not want to accept the fact that God is angry with sin. Instead, the fact that God is love is played for all it's worth. I agree that God is love, and the church certainly needs to learn to take the love of God into the marketplace of life. We have often failed to do that, but I feel that it has led to an overemphasis on the love of God in this generation. God is righteous, and God is holy, and God is just in what He does.

The question remains: How do you feel about your sin and God's anger toward it? Is it nothing to you? Jeremiah sat *weeping* over the city. There were not many others weeping with him. Oh, we are told in Psalm 137 that the captives who had been taken to Babylon sat down and wept when they remembered Zion. They cried out for vengeance, and I feel they had a perfect right to do that, but was there any genuine repentance? Or was it the repentance of a thief who is merely sorry he has been caught but does not repent of his thievery? The people who were carried into captivity wept. But Jeremiah, who did not go into captivity, wept also over the debris, the wreckage, the ashes, and ruins of the city. He was a free man, but he was moved, he was involved, and he was concerned.

Again, may I refer to the religious programs we have on television in our day. They are often finished, polished, and professional in their presentation. I think it is a credit to the church to do something in a professional way—that is good and right—but I am concerned that there was one word I did not hear: the word sin. Their message did not emphasize at all that God is righteous and He must punish our sin.

The virgin birth, the deity of Christ, His death and resurrection are all important, but the question is: Why did He die? That is the question raised in Psalm 22:1, "My God, my God, why hast thou forsaken me? . . ." Our Lord said that while He was hanging on the Cross. We find the answer to that question in the same psalm: "But thou art holy, O thou that inhabitest the praises of Israel" (Ps. 22:3, italics mine). He is holy. He is righteous. Christ died on that cross because you and I are sinners, hell-doomed sinners.

Look at the Cross today—"Is it nothing to you, all ye that pass by?" (v. 12). He didn't have to die. He suffered as no man has had to suffer. God forsook Him, but God will never forsake you as long as you live. He forsook Christ so that He would not have to forsake you. May I ask you, is it nothing to you?

McCheyne was a wonderful man of God in the past who had a real experience with the Lord. He wrote a poem about Jehovah-Tsidkenu, which means "the Lord our Righteousness" (see Jer. 23:6; 33:16), and Dr. H. A. Ironside quoted it in Notes on the Prophecy and Lamentations of Jeremiah (pp. 315, 316).

> I oft read with pleasure, to soothe or engage,
> Isaiah's wild measure, or John's simple page:
> But e'en when they pictured the blood-sprinkled
>   tree,
> Jehovah Tsidkenu was nothing to me.

Like tears from the daughters of Zion that roll,
I wept when the waters went over His soul;
Yet thought not that *my sins* had nailed to the tree
Jehovah Tsidkenu: 'twas nothing to me.

When free grace awoke me by light from on high,
Then legal fears shook me—I trembled to die.
No refuge, no safety in self could I see;
Jehovah Tsidkenu my Saviour must be.

My terrors all vanished before that sweet name;
My guilty fears banished, with boldness I came,
To drink at the fountain, life-giving and free;
Jehovah Tsidkenu *is all things to me.*

My friend, "Is it nothing to you, all ye that pass by?" Have you come to Jesus just to get a new personality? To bring a little peace into your soul, or to create a little love on your altar? Is *that* the reason He died on the Cross? Will you hear me, my friend? He died on the Cross to save you from *hell.*

The Holy Spirit has come into the world to reveal Christ as Savior, and He has come to convict the world of sin. What kind of sin? Murder? Thievery? Yes, but something is worse than that: they sinned ". . . *because they believe not on me*" (John 16:9, italics mine). God has a remedy for the thief. The thief on the cross was saved. I think Paul was guilty of murder, that he was responsible for the death of Stephen, but he got saved. Moses also was a murderer. God has a remedy for the murderer, the thief, and the liar, but God does not have a remedy for the man who rejects Jesus Christ. That is the greatest sin you can commit.

Rejection of Christ is a state rather than an act. You can never commit the act of rejecting Christ, but you can gradually come to the place where Christ and what He has done for you is absolutely meaningless. Jerusalem reached the place where God told Jeremiah, "Don't be disturbed that they are not listening to you. If Moses or Elijah or Samuel were here to pray for them, I would not answer their prayers either. It is too late; they have crossed over." There are many living in our so-phisticated day who have crossed over to that place.

Now we cannot judge when a man has reached the point of having totally rejected Christ. I have seen the conversion of many folk whom I'm sure I would have considered to be hopeless cases. One man I know of who lived in the San Francisco Bay area was on drugs and was guilty of several crimes, but he was marvelously and wonderfully converted. So neither you nor I are the ones to say that someone has stepped over that line, but it does happen.

Jerusalem had rejected God. An individual can reject God. What does Jesus Christ mean to you? What does His death mean to you? "Is it nothing to you, all ye that pass by?" (v. 12).

CHAPTER 2

THEME: Elegy 2

> **The Lord was as an enemy: he hath swallowed up Israel, he hath swallowed up all her palaces: he hath destroyed his strong holds, and hath increased in the daughter of Judah mourning and lamentation [Lam. 2:5].**

God took full responsibility for what Nebuchadnezzar did. God allowed him to destroy the city of Jerusalem. God used him as a rod, just as He had used the Assyrians against Israel for their punishment.

Have you ever stopped to think in your own personal life why God permits certain people to cross your path? Do you wish that you had never met certain people? Are there people whom you would call your enemies? Someone may have caused you sorrow, but it is all for His purpose. God has permitted all that for a definite purpose. Learn to recognize the hand of God in your life.

> **The Lord hath cast off his altar, he hath abhorred his sanctuary, he hath given up into the hand of the enemy the walls of her palaces; they have made a noise in the house of the LORD, as in the day of a solemn feast [Lam. 2:7].**

The very temple which God had blessed—He had given the instructions for building it, His very presence had been there at one time—now He says, "The day came that I abhorred that temple."

Churchgoing folk need to investigate their own lives. If you go to church, is that something that God takes delight in? Or is it actually something that hurts His cause? Is your frame of mind right when you go, or are you critical? Can the Spirit of God use you? I think that it can even be sinful to go to church. Do you know where the most dangerous place was the night Jesus was arrested? Was it down with that bunch of rascals who were plotting His death? No, my friend, the most dangerous place that night was in the Upper Room where Jesus was! Do you know why? *Satan* was there. He put it into the heart of Judas Iscariot to betray Him, and he also got into the heart of Simon Peter to deny Him. Just because you are going to church doesn't mean you are pleasing God.

> **The elders of the daughter of Zion sit upon the ground, and keep silence: they have cast up dust upon their heads; they have girded themselves with sackcloth: the virgins of Jerusalem hang down their heads to the ground [Lam. 2:10].**

All the people went through the outward gyrations of grief, but notice how Jeremiah was affected:

> **Mine eyes do fail with tears, my bowels are troubled, my liver is poured upon the earth, for the destruction of the daughter of my people; because the children and the sucklings swoon in the streets of the city [Lam. 2:11].**

"Mine eyes do fail with tears"—he cried so much he couldn't even see. "My bowels are troubled"—this thing tore him to pieces, it wrecked his health. He was involved; it broke his heart.

How many of us are willing to be really involved in God's work? Are we willing to endanger our health? Are we willing to give ourselves over to God?

> **All that pass by clap their hands at thee; they hiss and wag their head at the daughter of Jerusalem, saying, Is this the city that men call The perfection of beauty, The joy of the whole earth? [Lam. 2:15].**

The enemy without is elated at the misery of Jerusalem.

I am sometimes severe in my comments about the condition of the church in our day. I am retired from the active pastorate—although I am not retired from the work of God—and I need to ask myself how involved I am with my brethren who are in the ministry? When I see the problems in the church today, is it nothing to me? Do I just sit on the sidelines as a critic, or does it bring sorrow to my heart? I can say that I have been moved, and I want to be an encouragement to the many wonderful Bible-teaching pastors in our country. It is too easy to be harsh in our criticism when it means nothing to us at all.

CHAPTER 3

Each one of the chapters in this little Book of Lamentations forms an acrostic. That is, there are twenty-two letters in the Hebrew alphabet, and each of the twenty-two verses in each chapter begins with the succeeding letter. However, in this chapter there are sixty-six verses, which means that there are three verses that begin with each letter of the alphabet.

> **I am the man that hath seen affliction by the rod of his wrath.**
>
> **He hath led me, and brought me into darkness, but not into light.**
>
> **Surely against me is he turned; he turneth his hand against me all the day.**
>
> **My flesh and my skin hath he made old: he hath broken my bones [Lam. 3:1–4].**

This man Jeremiah has seen and gone through great trouble. His health is wrecked because of his concern for Jerusalem. Jeremiah was not unmoved by the destruction he had seen come to the nation. He did not run around saying, "I told you so!" Actually, he was heartbroken. His response also shows us how *God* feels. God is not removed; He goes with those who are His own. The Lord Jesus said, ". . . I will never leave thee, nor forsake thee" (Heb. 13:5). Whatever you are going through, you can be sure He is there.

> **This I recall to my mind, therefore have I hope.**
>
> **It is of the LORD'S mercies that we are not consumed, because his compassions fail not.**

They are new every morning: great is thy faithfulness.

The LORD is my portion, saith my soul; therefore will I hope in him [Lam. 3:21–24].

If I were to give a title to these last three chapters of Lamentations, it would be, "When Tomorrows Become Yesterdays." Jeremiah is now looking back upon the past. He had predicted the judgment that came upon Jerusalem, and Jeremiah sits in the rubble and ruin of Jerusalem weeping as he writes this lamentation.

These verses are the only bright spot in all of the five lamentations. "It is of the LORD'S mercies that we are not consumed, because his compassions fail not. They are new every morning: great is thy faithfulness." In spite of the severe judgment of God—and many thought it was too severe—Jeremiah can see the hand of God's mercy. They would have been utterly consumed had it not been for the mercy of God. If they had received their just deserts, they would have been utterly destroyed—they would have disappeared from the earth.

Was Judah's deliverance from such a fate due to something in them? No, it was all due to the *faithfulness* of God. He had promised Abraham that He would make a nation come from him—and this was the nation. He had promised Moses that He would put them into the land. He had promised Joshua that He would establish them there. He promised David that there would come One in his line to reign on the throne forever. The prophets all said that God would not utterly destroy this people but that He would judge them for their sin. God is faithful. He has judged them, but He will not utterly destroy them. A faithful remnant has always remained, and ultimately they will become a great nation again.

Will God judge America? A great many people think not, but I think He will.

CHAPTER 4

THEME: Elegy 4

This fourth lamentation is a meditation. Sitting amidst the debris and ashes of Jerusalem, Jeremiah describes the horror of the destruction of his city and the carrying into captivity of the people by Nebuchadnezzar. It is so terrifying that I might be tempted to shun giving such a doomsday message. But we need to face up to the fact that God is a righteous God as well as a God of love. God judges sin, and He is righteous in doing so. Judah did not receive full judgment because of the mercies of God. Habbakuk said, ". . . in wrath remember mercy" (Hab. 3:2). God never forgets to be merciful. There is always a way out for God's people if they will come God's way.

> **How is the gold become dim! how is the most fine gold changed! the stones of the sanctuary are poured out in the top of every street.**
>
> **The precious sons of Zion, comparable to fine gold, how are they esteemed as earthen pitchers, the work of the hands of the potter! [Lam. 4:1–2].**

Jeremiah is comparing gold to the young men of Zion. The fine young men of Judah who were like gold vessels are now like earthen vessels of clay. They have been broken. That is the terrifying thing about warfare: it eliminates the finest young men of a nation.

We are a proud people in this country. Even Christians are told that they need to think well of themselves. I heard of a Christian psychologist who teaches that you should get up every morning, look in the mirror, and say, "I love you!" Well, a lot of the saints don't need to be told that—they already love themselves! The apostle Paul says that we are not to think more highly of ourselves than we ought. If we don't think of ourselves more highly than we ought, we will find that we are merely clay vessels. In 2 Timothy Paul likens the believer to a clay vessel. However, the issue is not of what material the vessels are made, but how they are being used. Are we vessels for the Master's use or for our own use?

At the wedding in Cana of Galilee the Lord Jesus had the servants bring out those old beaten water pots, which had apparently been stuck back in a corner until after the wedding. He used those old pots to supply the crowd with drink. He could use those pots, but He had to fill them with water. The water is the Word of God. When we, as old water pots, get filled with the Word of God, God can use us.

The young men of Judah had not been serving God, and they were now just broken pieces of pottery. What a tragic picture this is!

> **The tongue of the sucking child cleaveth to the roof of his mouth for thirst: the young children ask bread, and no man breaketh it unto them [Lam. 4:4].**

The siege of Jerusalem by Nebuchadnezzar was a horrible thing. The people suffered inside the city. Instead of surrendering, they held out and saw their little babies die. Shakespeare has Lady Macbeth say: "I have given suck and know How tender 'tis to love the babe that milks me: I would, while it was smiling in my face, Have pluck'd my nipple from his boneless gums, And dash'd the brains out, had I so sworn as you" (*Macbeth*, Act 1, scene 7). That is a bitter awful thing! But don't point your finger back to the terrible things these people did, for today, my friend, abortion is the *murder* of little children.

> **They that did feed delicately are desolate in the streets: they that were brought up in scarlet embrace dunghills [Lam. 4:5].**

They had lived in luxury, they had had big supermarkets, but now the shelves of the supermarkets are bare. They no longer can enjoy the conveniences they once had—in fact, they don't have any at all.

Have you ever stopped to think what could happen to the place where you live? Suppose those supermarket shelves which now groan with food were all empty next week when you do your shopping. Suppose you flipped the switch in your home and the lights did not come on. Suppose there was no heat, no air conditioning, no gas for the automobile. A howl of despair would go up in this nation. We would be a helpless people. That's what happened to Jerusalem. God judged them.

For the punishment of the iniquity of the daughter of my people is greater than the punishment of the sin of Sodom, that was overthrown as in a moment, and no hands stayed on her [Lam. 4:6].

God judged Sodom and Gomorrah, but God judged Jerusalem more severely. Why was that? Because the sin of Jerusalem was worse than that of Sodom and Gomorrah. Sodom and Gomorrah were destroyed by homosexuality. That is an awful sin, but there is something worse than that. It is worse for a man to sit in the church pew and hear the gospel and do nothing about it. That might be true of someone reading this book. Jesus Christ died for you. God is merciful to you today, and you have turned your back on Him. When God judges, your judgment will be more severe than for the heathen in Africa or in the islands of the sea. Don't worry about the heathen out there; worry about yourself. How have you responded to God's offer of grace in Jesus Christ?

Her Nazarites were purer than snow, they were whiter than milk, they were more ruddy in body than rubies, their polishing was of sapphire [Lam. 4:7].

Boy, they looked good, didn't they? Religion today looks good. We have new churches today—new sanctuaries and nice Christian education buildings where we have a place to play volleyball and basketball. We've got a baseball team. We have a nice room for banquets. It all looks good on the outside. Now Jeremiah is saying that a Nazarite was one who took a voluntary oath, and many did it. They were complimented; they looked good, you know. But it was all on the outside;

their hearts were not changed. While it is wonderful to have beautiful churches—I'm not opposed to them; I'm excited about them—it is tragic when the people on the inside are not new creatures in Christ Jesus. They are still doing the same old sins. That is the picture Jeremiah gives us of the people of Judah.

> **They that be slain with the sword are better than they that be slain with hunger: for these pine away, stricken through for want of the fruits of the field [Lam. 4:9].**

Even though Jeremiah has witnessed the awful destruction of Jerusalem and those who had died, he says he would rather be dead than alive, for the condition of those who remained was so terrible.

> **The hands of the pitiful women have sodden their own children: they were their meat in the destruction of the daughter of my people [Lam. 4:10].**

The same thing took place when Titus destroyed Jerusalem in A.D. 70. The people got so hungry that mothers had to give their own babies to be eaten! We look back and think how horrible this was but today many mothers are having abortions, actually murdering their babies. If we don't want a baby, we must take responsibility for our actions before a baby becomes a reality. God has made us capable of having babies and when one has been conceived, it is His intention for that child to come into the world. The moment the child is conceived, he is a person and to abort a pregnancy is murder of a human being.

> **For the sins of her prophets, and the iniquities of her priests, that have shed the blood of the just in the midst of her [Lam. 4:13].**

Because the false prophets and the priests did not tell the people the truth, they were guilty of murder—that is God's estimate of it. A preacher who won't preach the Word of God and tell the people how they might be saved is put in this classification. *I* didn't say that—*God* said it. God says if you don't give out the Word of God, you are guilty.

The anger of the LORD hath divided them; he will no more regard them: they respected not the persons of the priests, they favoured not the elders [Lam. 4:16].

The people paid no attention to the priests who *were* giving out the Word of God. Jeremiah was a prophet of God, and they paid no attention to him at all. God judged the people for that.

As for us, our eyes as yet failed for our vain help: in our watching we have watched for a nation that could not save us [Lam. 4:17].

This is something the modern nation of Israel needs to learn. God did not put them back in the land in 1948; the *United Nations* made them a nation, and since that time they have never known one minute of peace. There have been wars and threats of war continually. They have not turned to God, and God did not put them back into the land.

Don't misunderstand me, I think the return of the Jews to Israel was a tremendous thing. Dr. W. F. Albright has made this statement: "It is without parallel in the annals of human history that a nation carried into captivity for seventy years should return to resume its national life, and that after nearly six hundred years, this same nation should again be scattered worldwide for nearly two thousand years and retain its identity." To see how God has dealt with this nation has caused many to turn to Him.

The Lord says that the problem was that Judah was looking to Egypt for help, and Egypt was *not* a help; they were an enemy. The United States should recognize that it is not the war machines we need to give to Israel. We need to give them the Word of God, the Word which they gave to us so many years ago.

The breath of our nostrils, the anointed of the LORD, was taken in their pits, of whom we said, Under his shadow we shall live among the heathen [Lam. 4:20].

What a picture of that people as they are today! They are scattered among the heathen.

The punishment of thine iniquity is accomplished, O daughter of Zion; he will no more carry thee away into captivity: he will visit thine iniquity, O daughter of Edom; he will discover thy sins [Lam. 4:22].

After the judgment, God promises that He will permanently place them in the land.

CHAPTER 5

THEME: Elegy 5

This fifth and final lamentation is a prayer of Jeremiah.

> **Remember, O LORD, what is come upon us: consider, and behold our reproach [Lam. 5:1].**

Judah had lost the honor and respect which she had had among the nations.

> **They ravished the women in Zion, and the maids in the cities of Judah.**
>
> **Princes are hanged up by their hand: the faces of elders were not honoured.**
>
> **They took the young men to grind, and the children fell under the wood [Lam. 5:11–13].**

Their women were ravished, and their princes hanged; they had lost everything. The young men who survived were put into slavery to work for Nebuchadnezzar.

> **The joy of our heart is ceased; our dance is turned into mourning [Lam. 5:15].**

The joy of their hearts had ceased.

> **Thou, O LORD, remainest for ever; thy throne from generation to generation.**
>
> **Wherefore dost thou forget us for ever, and forsake us so long time?**

Turn thou us unto thee, O Lord, and we shall be turned; renew our days as of old [Lam. 5:19–21].

This is the prayer of Jeremiah for his people. We could learn a lesson from this: before it is too late, we had better turn to the Lord.

Daniel Webster made this statement many years ago, and it sounds like a prophecy: "If religious books are not circulated among the masses and the people do not turn to God, I do not know what is to become of us as a nation. If truth be not diffused, error will be. If God and His Word are not received, the devil and his works will gain the ascendency. If the evangelical volume does not reach every hamlet, the pages of a corrupt and licentious literature will. If the power of the gospel is not felt through the length and the breadth of the land, anarchy, misrule, degradation, misery, corruption, and darkness will reign without mitigation or end." What a picture! We are living in a day when you cannot read the Bible in the schools, but pornography is permitted because we must be free to do what we want to do! Well, can't some of us have the Bible in our schools, especially when it is desired by the majority?

When our great nation was founded during the period from 1775 to 1787, the following statement by Benjamin Franklin was still widely accepted: "The longer I live the more convincing proofs I see of the truth that God governs in the affairs of men." Unless a marked change takes place in the United States of America, it's doomed just as sure as was ancient Babylon.

Dr. Machen said, "America is coasting downhill on a godly ancestry." Now we have reached the bottom of the hill. What a message Lamentations would have for us today, but it will not be selected as the Book of the Month or the Book of the Year. It is unfortunate that we will not listen.

(For Bibliography to Lamentations, see Bibliography at the end of Jeremiah.)